London with Kids

Alex and Gardê

To the many children whose research, thoughts and comments made this book theirs and not ours, and especially to Raphael

Peter Pan statue in
Kensington Gardens.

London is arguably the best city in the world for children. Nowhere ticks so many boxes as Britain's capital. The museums are fabulous and legion. And they are child friendly. Kids can sleep over with dinosaurs or mummies, fire rockets across the room, dress up as a Tudor or set the controls for Neptune and drift through the solar system in virtual 3D. The city's tourist sights offer thrills by the dozen. Kids can flee screaming from ghosts and ghouls, hurtle through a medieval maze, run down a bomb-blasted street during the Blitz, float over the city in a giant Ferris wheel, or whizz along the Thames in a jet boat. History comes alive at every turn, in romantic royal palaces, glorious gardens and magnificent mansions and monuments.

London is tranquil too. Parks proliferate; most have superb adventure playgrounds and acres of unspoilt space in which to play hide-and-seek or spread a picnic rug – wonderful on those long summer days that fade slowly into twilight. And when kids crave even wider open spaces there are plenty of sights within easy reach of the city – including the seaside, castles and Roman ruins and a string of Britain's most exciting theme parks and open-plan zoos.

Alex and Gardênia live in London. They have both been widely published. Alex was part of a team who won a US National Magazine Award in 2007 and is a runner-up in the FOE international photo competition. This is their third book for Footprint.

About the book

Children researched this book, not grown-ups

London with Kids is aimed at children of all ages. All the attractions are kids' favourites. In preparation for the guide we interviewed more than 200 children, both ourselves and in collaboration with Brooklands Primary School in London, to discover what kids love best in the capital. You'll find their comments throughout the text, and all the sights we include have been vetted not only by adults but by the children we consulted too. We discovered so much along the way, including that children are interested in a far greater diversity of things than we adults give them credit for. Some love stately homes and museums far more than theme park rides and many liked the parks as much or more than the zoos. We had plenty of surprises too.

Our own son was our greatest guide. We saw London through seven-year-old Raphael's eyes. After enjoying the costly rides at Legoland, the heights of the London Eye, the lavish rooms of Hampton Court and the thrills and scares of the London Dungeon he told us that his favourite thing to do in London was to ride the public boat to Greenwich – one of the capital's cheapest thrills. Why? "because you can really feel the spirit of the sea and it makes me feel happy."

We hope your tots, toddler and teens help you to discover surprising parts of London too and that our book will give you some ideas.

Age appropriate

We feel strongly that parents are the best judges of what is or is not appropriate or interesting for their kids. Whilst we provide guidelines for some of the scarier sights, we have not decided for you what is or is not suitable. Kids' tastes are so diverse and surprising that we simply do not feel qualified to second guess.

London areas

We have separated London into areas and added a chapter of suggested excursions. Dividing the city thus will always be an inexact exercise, especially as west and east London both stretch north and south of the river. The areas we have chosen are as follows:

Central London – this covers the big sights in Westminster, the City of London, Chelsea and Kensington and the South Bank in Southwark.

North London – which covers everything north of Marylebone Road, including big sights like Madame Tussaud's.

South London – whilst we have stolen the South Bank (where you'll find the London Eye, Tower Bridge and Tate) from south London and put it in Central London, this area covers everything south of the Thames, east of Wimbledon and west of Greenwich.

West London – here we include everything west of Kensington to the north of the Thames and west Wimbledon to the south of the river.

East London – this covers the area east of the City of London (both north and south of the Thames).

Excursions – there is so much to see in easy reach of the city that we have included a pot pourri of favourites as well as resources which will help parents explore further.

Eating & sleeping

Our guide is small enough to fit in a coat pocket and yet filled with scores of photos, which make it perfect for armchair reading. There are plenty of restaurant ideas in the back of the book and information on how to find a good London hotel, but space was limited and we have prioritized the sights, which are covered more thoroughly and extensively than in any other London kids' guide.

Contents

Top 10

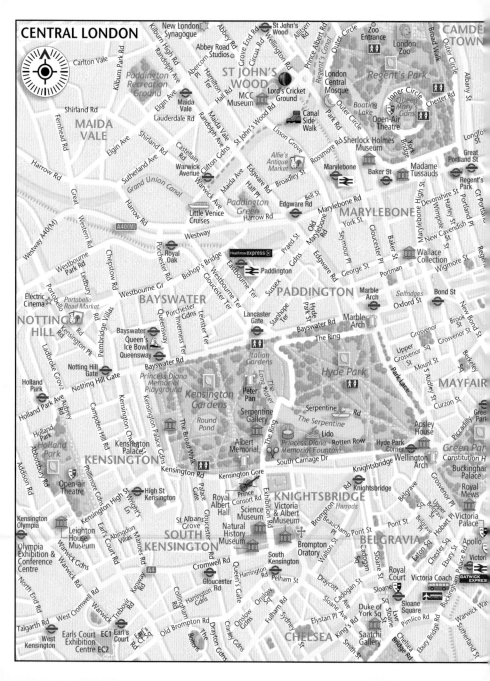

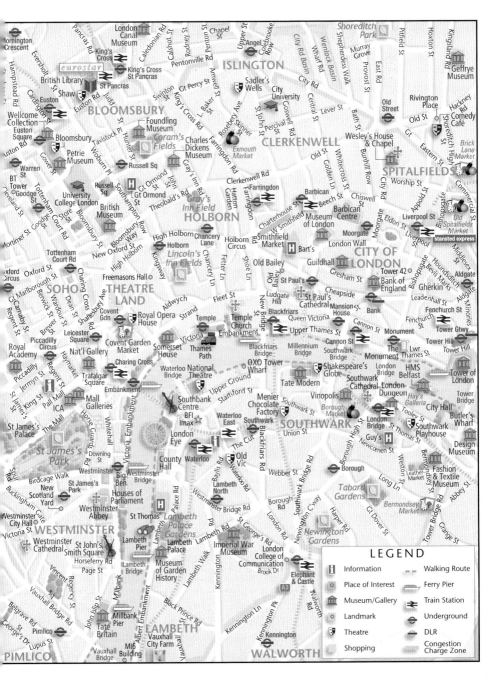

Festivals & events calendar

January

London Parade (New Year's Day; londonparade.co.uk). Britain's biggest annual procession, with more than 10,000 performers marching bands, majorettes and horse-drawn carriages.

Chinese New Year (late Jan/early Feb). Parades of paper dragons, firecrackers and general celebrations around Gerrard Street in Chinatown.

February

London Fashion Week (late Feb; londonfashionweek.co.uk). Catwalk shows from the world's best designers and a spate of associated fashion events.

Shrove Tuesday (Feb/Mar). Pancake races at Spitalfields and around Covent Garden.

March

St Patrick's Day Parade (Sun closest to St Patrick's Day). Marching bands, floats, street theatre, music and a procession in Central London (usually between Green Park and Trafalgar Square), from all 32 Irish counties, dressed in their traditional colours.

East Festival (early Mar; visitlondon. com/events/east/). A six-day celebration of the multicultural life of east London, with British South Asian art shows, family events at the Barbican and free concerts.

Head of the River Race (last weekend in Mar; horr.co.uk). London's largest and most spectacular rowing race, with some 400 boats from makeshift tubs to state-of-the-art sculls.

Oxford and Cambridge Boat Race (end Mar; theboatrace.org). Britain's most prestigious universities go head to head in a race along the Thames. A great excuse for a picnic on the river.

April

London Marathon (Sun in mid-Apr; virginlondonmarathon.com). Hundreds of thousands gather in central London to see the world's best athletes compete alongside amateurs dressed in odd costumes.

St George's Day (23 Apr). England's national day is celebrated with free events (cabaret, comedy and theatre) around Trafalgar Square and a St George's Day rugby match at Twickenham.

May

Brighton Festival (brightonfestival. org). One of the biggest arts festivals in Europe with a host of events for kids.

May Fayre & Puppet Festival (Sun closest to 9 May; alterntativearts. co.uk). All manner of puppetry in and around Covent Garden, including dozens of traditional Punch and Judy shows.

Chelsea Flower Show (end May; rhs. org.uk/Shows-Events). The biggest annual celebration of the English garden is held in a huge space next to the Thames. The Royal Family and more than 160,000 others attend.

Coin Street Festival (end May; coinstreet.org). Music theatre and kids' events on the South Bank.

June

City of London Festival (Jun–Jul; colf. org). Free concerts, street theatre and dance during the day and paid-for concerts in the evenings all over the City.

The Scoop (mid-Jun; morelondon. com). An 800-seat temporary amphitheatre is set up next to City Hall on the Thames with free film, theatre, music, kids' performances and community events.

Spitalfields Summer Festival (mid-Jun; spitalfieldsfestival.org.uk). Classical music, singing and assorted arts and performance events in the old market.

West End Live (mid-Jun; westendlive.co.uk). Edited versions of London's musicals and plays are shown for free in Leicester Square, together with small exhibits from the Science Museum, V&A and others.

July

Trooping the Colour (early Jul; trooping-the-colour.co.uk). A series of elaborate, brightly coloured military displays take place at Horse Guards Parade in front of the Queen to celebrate her official birthday. There's also a fly past down the Mall by the RAF. Apply for tickets through a ballot in the January and February preceding the show by writing to The Brigade Major, Headquarters Household Division, Horse Guards, Whitehall, London SW1A 2AX, T020-7413 2479.

Hampton Court Flower Show (early Jul; rhs.org.uk). The world's largest annual flower show is held in the palace gardens with stunning floral displays, workshops and stalls.

Hayes Carnival (early Jul; hillingdon.gov.uk). One of the biggest London street parades with dozens of free events, from live music to street performance.

BBC Proms (mid-Jul; bbc.co.uk). The Henry Wood Promenade concerts have been performed in London since 1895. There are some 100 shows each year, most held in the evening in the Royal Albert Hall (royalalberthall.com), but also at Cadogan Hall and al fresco in London's parks. The Last Night of the Proms is a national event, with hundreds of revellers – many of them waving Union Jack flags for a concert of bombastic British classical music. Prom concerts are very child-friendly but book well ahead for the Last Night, as there is a very high demand for tickets.

Doggett's Coat & Badge Race (mid-Jul; watermenshall.org). This is said to be the oldest rowing race in the world. It's very colourful and attracts a lively crowd along the Thames.

August
Notting Hill Carnival (Aug bank hol, thenottinghillcarnival.com). Europe's biggest street festival can get a bit overwhelming for small kids, who are easily frightened by the huge crowds. Older children, however, will love the colourful costumes, drums and parades.

England's Medieval Festival (last weekend Aug). Jousting, medieval pageantry, falconry, long-bow shooting and a big medieval battle in the grounds of Herstmonceux Castle in Sussex.

September
Thames Festival (early Sep; thames festival.org). London's biggest end-of-the-summer party with concerts, a carnival, circuses, firework displays, markets and street performances.

Clarence House Garden Party (from 8 Sep; startuk.org). Prince Charles hosts an 11-day knees-up in the gardens of his London palace to raise money for his favourite charities.

Great River Race (mid-Sep; greatriverrace.co.uk). River craft – from adapted bath tubs and Polynesian war canoes to svelte competition kayaks – race the Thames.

Heritage Open Days (mid-Sep or Oct; heritageopendays.org.uk). A weekend event that sees historic buildings throughout England open to visitors. A week later, a similar programme called the **Open House** project (openhouselondon.org.uk) takes place in London.

Epping Forest Festival (Sun in early Sep; www.cityoflondon.gov. uk). Jousting on Chingford plain, barbecues, crossbow shooting and medieval pageantry, fun and games.

October
Punch and Judy Festival (early Oct; punchandjudyfellowship.org. uk). Dozens of Punch and Judy and similar shows from all across Europe perform in Covent Garden.

Halloween (31 Oct). Trick or treating throughout London and spooky kids' nights at many of the attractions, including a Halloween Show at the London Dungeon (page 36) and a ghostly canal cruise through the canal museum (page 97).

November
Lord Mayor's Show (lordmayorsshow. org). The Lord Mayor of London climbs into a golden carriage and joins the world's oldest civic procession from the City of London to the Royal Courts of Justice. Thousands gather to watch and there's a huge fireworks display afterwards.

Bonfire Night (5 Nov). The annual celebration of the foiling of the Gunpowder Plot sees fireworks and bonfires lit all over the capital. The biggest are on Clapham Common and Alexandra Park.

December
New Year's Eve. London hosts one of the biggest parties in the world with a 10-minute cascade of multicoloured fireworks that floods over the London Eye, bursts from boats on the Thames and lights up the Houses of Parliament and Westminster Abbey. This is not an event for smaller children as the crowds get very big and toilet facilities are few and far between.

London's markets

London has dozens of street markets; many have a long history and each has a character of its own. They are great places to stock up on picnic foods, buy souvenirs or just have a browse. The bustle, variety and colour invariably interest children and make a good excuse to get out of the museums and sample a bit of life on a London street.

Central London

Berwick Street Berwick St, W1, Mon-Sat 0900-1700, tube: Tottenham Court Road or Leicester Square.
This colourful local market is a great place to stock up on fruit for a picnic, with huge bags of berries, apples and pears, citrus and tropical delights selling for as little as a pound.

Borough SE1, boroughmarket.org.uk, Thu 1100-1700, Fri 1200-1800, Sat 0900-1600, tube: Borough or London Bridge.
Middle-class Londoners and now, increasingly, tourists flock to Borough Market to buy artisan cheeses, breads, organic olive oils and similar and to sip caffè macchiato in smart cafés. Come for lunch or to shop for a picnic after a stroll along the nearby South Bank; food here is far better value and higher quality than in the chain restaurants along the river.

Cabbages & Frocks St Marylebone Parish Church, Marylebone High St, W1, cabbagesandfrocks.co.uk, Sat 1100-1700, tube: Baker Street.
London's newest market has some 40 stalls of expensive but high-quality food and drink, cosmetics, clothing and accessories. Come here to buy picnic supplies before heading to nearby Regent's Park. The market runs a Summer Fayre and a children's day in May.

Covent Garden Covent Garden Piazza, daily 1030-1930, tube: Covent Garden.
This once shambolic fruit and vegetable market has been transformed in the last 50 years to become one of central London's retail capitals. It can be hard even to find the remnants of the original market, but they are here: the Apple Market (just off the piazza between Tavistock and Henrietta streets) sells antiques on Mondays and upmarket arts, crafts, bric-a-brac, toys and clothing during the rest of the week. The larger Jubilee Market on the piazza is more touristy, selling crafts, smelly soaps, cosmetics, junk and jewellery and antiques on Monday. See also page 70.

Smithfields Charterhouse St, EC1A, smithfieldmarket.com, Mon-Fri 0400-1200, tube: Farringdon.
This huge market is worth visiting in passing, if only for the splendid old Victorian wrought iron and the serried ranks of bright red London phone boxes. It's the last wholesale market in the city to continue on its original site. Meat has been sold at Smithfields for over 800 years.

North London

Camden markets Daily 1000-1900 but busiest on Sat, tube: Camden Town or Chalk Farm.
Camden's many markets sprawl around Regent's Canal and are an immensely popular bastion of London's mainstream alternative culture. Come here for quirky toys, gifts and greetings cards, CDs, incense and posters, as well as second-hand and designer cast-off clothes, hippy tie-dye and a huge range of imported Asian, South American and African craft items

and textiles, most of which are of dubious quality. Expect big crowds of teenaged and young tourists at weekends, many of them dressed in club party gear and daubed with tribal tattoos, which can easily be acquired in Camden in temporary or permanent form. There are numerous stalls selling cheap food and better quality restaurants close to Camden Town tube.

West London

Portobello Road W10, Mon-Wed and Fri-Sat 0800-1830, tube: Notting Hill Gate or Ladbroke Grove.
This mile-long market, which gets almost unbearably crowded on a summer Saturday afternoon, sells all manner of antiques (Fri and Sat only), arts, crafts and vintage clothing. The street itself is lined with fashion shops, cafés and restaurants.

East London

Billingsgate Fish Market North Quay, West India Dock, E14, Tue-Sat 0500-0830, DLR: West India Quay.
Billingsgate has been trading for nearly 1000 years, though not at these premises, which lie a stone's throw from Canary Wharf in a vast, smelly warehouse. If your children are early risers, bring them to see fish of every conceivable variety, plus huge lobsters, crabs and prawns.

Brick Lane Brick Lane and Bethnal Greed Rd, E1, Sun 0600-1300, tube: Liverpool Street, rail: Shoreditch.
The main market sells bric-a-brac of every kind, with hundreds of fly pitchers flogging second-hand wares on the streets. Higher-end arts and crafts and kids' clothes are proffered at the Sunday Upmarket

(sundayupmarket.co.uk, Sun 1000-1700), in a car park off Brick Lane between Buxton and Wood Seer Streets. There are also designer togs, crafts and hand-made toys at the Backyard Market (next to the Atlantic Gallery in front of the Vibe Bar, Sat 1100-1800).

Columbia Road Columbia Rd, east of Ravenscroft St to Barnet Grove, E2, Sun 0800-1330, tube: Old Street or Bethnal Green.
Lined with pretty gift shops and cafés, Columbia Road is the venue for a flower market every Sunday. It's increasingly popular with London's chattering classes so come early to avoid the worst crowds.

Greenwich Church St, Stockwell St and Greenwich High Rd, SE10, Wed 0930-1700 (food court), Thu 0930-1700 (antiques), Fri 0900-1700 (crafts), Sat-Sun 0930-1700 (general), DLR: Cutty Sark, rail: Greenwich.
This string of large markets sells everything from high-quality food and drink to antiques, curios and toys. Sundays can be very busy; Saturdays offer the same choice but are far quieter.

Petticoat Lane Wentworth St and around, E1, Mon-Fri 1000-1430, Sun 0900-1400, tube: Aldgate, Aldgate East or Liverpool Street.
Once an old Victorian rag market, come to Petticoat Lane for all manner of clothes – from fashion boutique seconds to trendy T-shirts – and cheap toys, with the occasional gem turning up in a sea of cheap Chinese plastic.

Ridley Road Ridley Rd between Kingsland High St and St Mark's Rise, E8, Mon-Sat from 0900, rail: Dalston Kingsland or Hackney Downs.
London's biggest Caribbean market proffers all manner of tropical fruits, vegetables and foods, as well as CDs of Jamaican music, clothes and arts and crafts.

Spitalfields Commercial St, visitspitalfields.com, Thu 0700-1500 (antiquities, curios and crafts), Fri 1000-1700 (crafts), Sun 1000-1700 (main market), tube: Liverpool Street.
This covered market is one of London's most popular, especially on a Sunday. Here you'll find books, clothes, antiques and dozens of stalls of browsable bric-a-brac, including toys. The market has a wealth of cafés and restaurants for refreshment, including a branch of kids' favourite, Giraffe (see page 180).

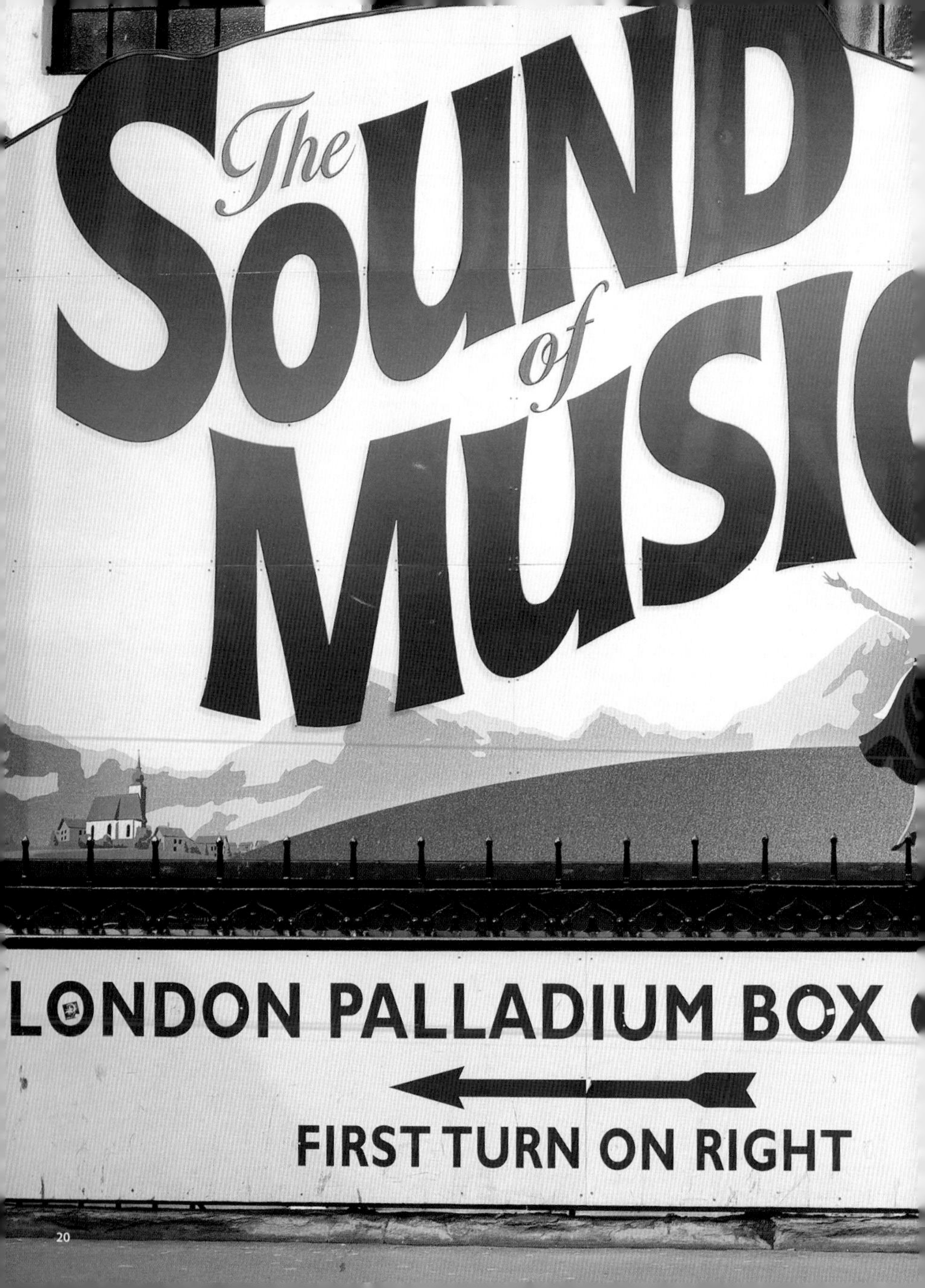
The
SOUND
of
MUSI
LONDON PALLADIUM BOX
FIRST TURN ON RIGHT

West End shows

London offers the best theatre and musicals in the world and a night out at a West End show is a real kids' treat. New productions begin every few months, so it's always worth checking the **Visit London** (visitlondon. com) and **Official London Theatre** (officiallondontheatre. co.uk) websites for the latest, but there are also a number of long-running shows that are particularly popular with children. The **Lion King** (Lyceum Theatre, Wellington St, WC2E, T0844-844 0005, disney. co.uk/musicaltheatre, £20-65, tube: Covent Garden) is a stage adaptation of the famous Disney rite-of-passage cartoon, with fabulous costumes and stunning sets, and is suitable for children of all ages. **Les Misérables** (Queen's Theatre, Shaftesbury Av, W1D, T0844-8471607, lesmis.com, £15-60, tube: Leicester Square) is a moving adaptation of Victor Hugo's 19th-century social realist classic and has been immensely popular for well over 20 years. The show's Kids' Club includes a backstage tour. Newcomers that look set to be on stage for quite some time include the Broadway hit, **Shrek** (Theatre Royal, Drury Lane, Catherine St, WC2B, T0844-4825138, shrekthemusical. co.uk, £17.50-65, tube: Covent Garden), a musical adaptation

of the Dreamworks cartoon about a grumpy ogre who finds his true love and saves the kingdom, and Andrew Lloyd Webber's sequel to **The Phantom of the Opera**, **Love Never Dies** (Adelphi Theatre, Strand, WC2E, T0844-412 4651, reallyuseful.com, £27.10-73.25, tube: Charing Cross or Covent Garden), which is good for kids over seven.

There's plenty of more serious theatre for kids too, especially from designated children's theatres Polka Dot (polkadottheatre.com) and Half Moon (halfmoon.org.uk); for others, see pages 97 and 117. And, look out for Kids Week (dates vary; kidsweek. co.uk), during which a five- to 16-year-old can watch a show for free when accompanied by a paying adult; parents can also buy up to two further kids' tickets at half price. There's wonderful opera and ballet too, with something for kids every season at the **Royal Opera House** (roh.org.uk), Sadler's Wells (sadlerswells. com) or the **English National Opera** (eno.org).

> **❝❞**
> A good thing to do is to see a panto. You can say funny things. It makes you express your feelings. A panto is like a play but you say stuff like 'It's behind you!'
>
> **Serena, aged 8**

River Thames

London is defined by the River Thames. This was the city's principal thoroughfare until the 20th century and history crowds its banks. Queens and courtiers entered the Tower of London by boat through the Traitors' Gate; Henry VIII sailed between Westminster and Hampton Court, and Shakespeare's Globe, the Queen's House in Greenwich, the Houses of Parliament and the glistening spires of the modern City of London all overlook the river. Even today, one of the best ways to see the city is by boat.

Thames Clippers (T020-7001 2222, thamesclippers.com, £5.50 adult, £2.80 child, free under 5s, for various discounts see site) are much the best and best-value option, with a fleet of fast catamarans, which run every 20 minutes between piers at the London Eye and the O2 centre (with numerous hop-on-and-off stops along the way). The boats reach exciting speeds; sit out on deck at the back for the most exhilarating ride and the best views. **City Cruises** (citycruises. com, adult from £13, £6.50 child) run cruises between the Houses of Parliament and Bermondsey, taking in sights just beyond Tower Bridge and have commentators famous for their witty repartee. They also have dinner cruises with food of sketchy quality. Other companies offering the same or a similar route include **London Eye**

Cruises (londoneye.com, £12, £6 child, under 4s free, combination tickets with the London Eye and other Merlin Entertainments attractions available) and **Circular Cruise Westminster** (The Old Pump House, Blackfriars Pier, EC4V 3QR, T020-7936 2033, single £8, £4 child, return £10.50, £5.25 child).

More popular with children are the **London Duck Tours** (55 York Rd, SE1 7NJ, T020-7928 3132, londonducktours.co.uk, £20, £16 13-17s, £14 under 13s, only 2 infants per tour) and the exhilarating **Rigid Inflatable Boat** (RIB) cruises. The former explore Westminster by street and river in an amphibious World War II vehicle. The latter offer an adrenalin rush along the river from central London all the way to the Thames Barrier. Companies offering RIB tours include **Flying Fish** (Kings Reach/Victoria Embankment, City of London, E1W, T0844-991 5050, flyingfishtours.co.uk, summer only), which departs from St Katherine's pier (next to Tower Bridge), and **London RIB Voyages** (Boarding Gate 1, Millennium Pier SE1, T020-7928 8933, londonribvoyages.com). RIB cruises are safe for children of all ages.

If you prefer to stay on dry land, note that the **Thames Path** traces the route of the river, passing, close to many iconic sights (see pages 32 and 116).

Celebrity & film tours

You can see celebrity homes and locations in London with the **Celebrity Planet** bus tours (thecelebrityplanet.com, 90 mins, £25). They visit homes owned or lived in by celebs like Madonna, Winston Churchill, Princess Diana, Jimi Hendrix and Oscar Wilde and film locations including those from the Harry Potter and James Bond films. **Walks.com** offers Harry Potter film location walking tours in central London at weekends, costing around £3. The **London Taxi Tour** (londontaxitour.com) provides a range of Harry Potter tours in black cabs costing from £390 for four people, visiting London sights together with those in Oxford and Lacock.

Funfairs

London's parks host scores of annual funfairs. There's bound to be one on when you visit. You can find out where by looking on visitlondon.com or irvinleisure.co.uk.

Blue plaques

Look out for blue plaques on London's buildings. They mark a spot where a famous or important person lived. They include Mahatma Gandhi, Winston Churchill, Sir Isaac Newton, Sigmund Freud, Bob Marley and Vincent van Gogh. You can find an almost complete list of plaques on Wikipedia.

Parrots in the park

Try and spot the feral parakeets in the London's parks. They're ring-necked parakeets native to sub-Saharan Africa and India. They probably escaped from film studios or arrived as castaways on cargo ships. There are also terrapins in the ponds in Hampstead Heath and yellow-tailed scorpions on the dockside in Sheerness in Kent.

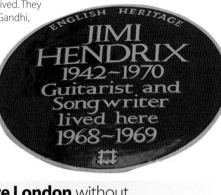

ENGLISH HERITAGE
JIMI HENDRIX
1942~1970
Guitarist and Songwriter lived here 1968~1969

Don't leave London without...

Seeing a wild deer in Richmond Park

Trying to make a sentry at Horse Guards Parade giggle

Riding in a London rickshaw

Taking a boat on the Thames

Spotting a raven at the Tower of London

Straddling the longitude line at Greenwich

Firing a rocket in the Science Museum

Posing for a photo on the lions in Trafalgar Square

Spotting the skull in Holbein's *Ambassadors* painting in the National Gallery

Whispering in the dome of St Paul's

Finding a Harry Potter film location

Can you find...

- Princess Diana's memorial fountain and playground in Kensington Gardens?

- The Buddhist Pagoda in Battersea Park?

- The world's smallest police station on the southeast corner of Trafalgar Square?

- The MI6 spy headquarters on the Thames next to Vauxhall Bridge?

- The coats of arms of Henry VIII's wives in the great hall at Hampton Court?

- Dick Whittington's cat on the Whittington Stone Memorial on Highgate Hill?

- Peter Pan's statue in Kensington Gardens?

- Llamas in Golder's Hill Park?

- The zebra crossing in St John's Wood made famous by the Beatles?

- A pet cemetery near the Victoria Gates in Hyde Park?

What's the connection?

Who or what connects the following London landmarks?

★ St Jude the Martyr church, London Zoo, Australia House and King's Cross station

★ Fleet Street, the Strand and Trafalgar Square

★ Morden, Bank and Camden Town

★ Buckingham, Kensington, St James's, Westminster and Hampton Court

★ London Eye, HMS Belfast, Hampton Court and Tower Bridge

Answers on page 184.

Who am I?

Can you work out who these famous Londoners are from the clues below?

- ❷ I live at No 11 Downing Street
- ❷ I look down on London from Trafalgar Square
- ❷ I wrote about more gruel, Christmas ghosts and the Artful Dodger
- ❷ I lived and didn't live at 221b Baker Street
- ❷ I was found on a London railway platform and love marmalade
- ❷ I made meat pies out of my customers
- ❷ I arrived in London looking for streets paved with gold
- ❷ I governed London from a secret bunker in Whitehall during a war
- ❷ I celebrate my birthday twice every year
- ❷ Two of my wives lost their heads over me

Answers on page 184.

Make your own
Chelsea bun

These currant buns were first baked in the 18th century in a famous bakers and bun house in Chelsea. The recipe has diversified since. Here is one of the simplest. The buns are most delicious when served with hot chocolate.

Ingredients
225 g flour
1 tsp salt
112 g butter
100 g caster sugar
25 g yeast
250 ml warm milk
4 eggs
150 g currants
1 tsp mixed spice

Method
❶ Mix the flour and salt then blend in half the butter using your fingers until the mixture feels like breadcrumbs. Add the sugar.

❷ Mash the yeast to make it creamy, mix it with warm milk, whisk the eggs into the milk and yeast mix.

❸ Scoop a hole in the middle of the flour and pour in the mix. Use your fingers to mix it together and rub it until smooth.

❹ Leave for 90 minutes until the mix expands to double its size.

❺ Knead gently on a board covered in flour and then shape the dough into a square covering the whole board.

❻ Sprinkle the dough with sugar, then soften the rest of the butter and spread it onto the dough. Fold and roll out again.

❼ Cover the flattened dough evenly with fruit and spice. Sprinkle a little more sugar over the top then roll up the flattened dough like a carpet.

❽ Cut the roll into 5 cm slices. Lie these next to each other on a greased baking tin. Cover the slices with a damp tea towel and put them in a warm oven (40°C) for 15-20 minutes.

❾ Remove the slices and sprinkle with sugar.

❿ Return them to the oven and bake at 200°C until risen and lightly brown.

⓫ Remove and allow to cool.

Ten children's books set in London

A Bear called Paddington
Michael Bond (Harper Collins)
A bear from darkest Peru stows away and is found by Mr and Mrs Brown in a box at Paddington railway station. The bear's subsequent adventures often involve marmalade.

The BFG
Roald Dahl (Puffin)
The Big Friendly Giant and Sophie visit the capital, walking across busy Hyde Park Corner and popping into Buckingham Palace.

The Diamond of Drury Lane
Julia Golding (Egmont Books)
The first of a series of historical novels for girls following the exploits of Cat Royal, a little girl who lives in the Theatre Royal in the 18th century.

The Enemy
Charles Higson (Puffin)
A band of brave children fight a world of mad cannibal adults around Buckingham Palace and numerous famous London sights. For kids who love the London Dungeon.

Katie in London
James Mayhew (Orchard)
One of a series of lovely picture books for two-year-olds and older, in which Katie visits the big London sights with her Grandma and meets a magical stone lion in Trafalgar Square.

King of Shadows
Susan Cooper (Red Fox)
A modern boy, Nat Field, is transported to Shakespeare's Globe Theatre, where he meets the bard, acts in his plays and has a series of rip-roaring adventures.

Mortal Engines
Philip Reeve (Scholastic)
A boy struggles to return to a living, moving London which wanders around the globe literally consuming other cities.

The Phoenix and the Carpet
E Nesbit (Puffin)
An early 20th-century classic full of evocative descriptions of Edwardian London, in which brothers and sisters have adventures with a phoenix and a magical carpet.

Smith
Leon Garfield (Puffin)
A Dickensian adventure story set in 18th-century London, following the adventures of a wily 12-year-old pickpocket and a host of colourful London characters.

The Wombles
Elizabeth Beresford (Bloomsbury)
The adventures of a burrow of furry creatures who keep Wimbledon Common tidy by making use of the rubbish left behind by humans.

Contents

Central London

The London Eye.

You must

❶ Marvel at the view from the London Eye.

❷ Quake and scream in the London Dungeon.

❸ Tremble at the Tyrannosaurus in the Natural History Museum.

❹ Picnic near a palace in one of the royal parks.

❺ Watch wildlife at dusk along the banks of the Serpentine.

❻ Fire rockets and solve puzzles in the Science Museum.

❼ Spend a night in the British or Natural History Museum.

❽ Rollick and roar with pirates on the *Golden Hinde*.

❾ Paint a masterpiece at the National Gallery.

❿ Cruise through the city by boat.

Central London is home to the city's flagship sights: Tower Bridge and the Tower of London, the London Eye, the British and Natural History museums all lie here, alongside the architectural relics of Britain's centuries of global power. The area grew from two discrete cities, which remain distinct and different in character to this day.

The **City of London**, which bristles with skyscrapers and fills with suits and money in the morning market rush, is where the capital was born, growing from a Stone Age settlement on a marsh to a Roman fort and a Norman city which cowed under the hulking presence of the Tower of London. The **City of Westminster**, which clusters around the great buildings of state – the Houses of Parliament, the government offices of Whitehall and the seat of monarchical power at St James's and Buckingham palaces – was where the kings and queens of old England chose to reside, close to what were once royal hunting grounds and are now a string of magnificent semi-wooded royal parks that are perfect for a breath of fresher air or a picnic. This is the London of films and photographs: a city of palaces and great monuments, encrusted with gargoyles and imbued with imperial pomp, clustered along the turbid Thames. But it also encompasses the bright lights of Piccadilly Circus and Leicester Square and the endless commercial bustle of Oxford and Regent streets.

London can be tiring for small feet and the crowds are overwhelming in summer, especially on the tube. The most restful way of getting to many places is along the great conduit which has long linked the two cities, the River Thames. Public boats cruise between the Houses of Parliament and the City, and the Thames Path runs along the river's bank, offering space, air and light.

The Great Court at the British Museum.

Out & about South Bank & Southwark

The South Bank offers a pick and mix of top London tourist attractions, all within walking distance of each other along one of the most spectacular stretches of the Thames. The London Eye, *Golden Hinde*, Aquarium and Tate Modern all lie here, as do the scream-inducing London Dungeon and London Bridge Experience. Expect crowds, high prices and tired kids at the end of the day.

Fun & free

Be a culture vulture

The regeneration of the south bank of the Thames began with the construction of the **Southbank Centre** (Belvedere Rd, SE1 8XX, southbankcentre.co.uk, tube: Waterloo), a brutalist conglomeration of galleries and concert halls, to mark the Festival of Britain in 1951. It is now one of Europe's largest centres for the arts. There are five principal organizations in the centre – the Royal Festival Hall, the Queen Elizabeth Hall, the Purcell Room, the Hayward Gallery and the Poetry Library – which, between them, annually host some thousand paid performances of music, dance and literature, up to six major art exhibitions, around 300 free foyer events and numerous workshops, many of which take place at lunchtime or in the afternoon, with plenty on offer for kids. The **National Theatre** (T020-7452 3000, nationaltheatre.org.uk) and the **British Film Institute** (Belvedere Rd, SE1, T020-7928 3232, bfi.org.uk, Tue-Sun 1200-2000) are both contiguous with the Southbank Centre. The latter's Mediatheque room has an enormous archive of children's TV and film classics, alongside plenty for adults, all viewable for free on large computer screens. Nearby is the **BFI IMAX** (1 Charlie Chaplin Walk, SE1 8XR, T0871-787 2525, imax.com).

Stroll along the Thames

The 5½ miles of the **Thames Path** (see also South London

The Royal Festival Hall is where very famous musicians perform their music like Nigel Kennedy and Vanessa Mãe. Also you can hire the royal box for a very special treat!

Lewis, aged nine

page 116) between Westminster and Tower bridges are by far the most popular stretch of this 184-mile river footpath. There are few urban river walks more scenic anywhere in the world. Westminster Bridge leads directly to the **Palace of Westminster** (see page 51), which towers over the north bank of the river; the path passes under the bridge and immediately past a host of sights clustered in and around the old **County Hall** building. Stop off to see the sharks and seahorses in the **Aquarium** (see page 36), Darth Vader in the **Film Museum** (see page 39) or the views from the **London Eye**, before having photos snapped with the many street performers and living statues who ply their trade a few hundred metres east around the **Jubilee Gardens**. There's usually a magic roundabout here, ice cream vans and candyfloss on sale, and the gardens themselves have a (well-tramped) lawn for a possible picnic and a children's playground. The **Southbank Centre** (see page 32) lies a little beyond at Waterloo Bridge, under which there is a daily second-hand book market (open until 1900). Teens who like to skate should bring a board to join in at the popular skateboard park underneath the Southbank Centre's Queen Elizabeth Hall.

The Thames Path continues past the shops, restaurants and pubs of **Gabriel's Wharf** (coin street.org) and the iconic **OXO Tower** (with its plush restaurant with a view) to Blackfriars Bridge. There are wonderful views east from here towards St Paul's and the City. Blackfriars tube and rail station is on the north bank for those with tired feet, or there are still more attractions further east. Between Blackfriars and London bridges you'll find the **Tate Modern** (see page 37), **Shakespeare's Globe** (see page 40), the **Clink Prison Museum** (see page 39), **Golden Hinde** (see page 39) and **Borough Market** (see page 16). It's only 15 minutes' walk from here to **Tower Bridge** (see page 42), the **London Bridge Experience** (see page 36), **London Dungeon** (see page 36), **HMS Belfast** (see page 40) and the **Scoop**, an amphitheatre outside the Mayor of London's City Hall headquarters.

Harry spotter

Harry flies along the **River Thames** on his broomstick past the London Eye, Houses of Parliament and Tower Bridge in *The Order of the Phoenix*. You can enjoy similar views from the Thames Path between Westminster and Tower bridges. (Tube: Tower Hill or Westminster)

The **Millennium Bridge** between Tate Modern and St Paul's is destroyed by the Death Eaters in *The Half Blood Prince*. (Tube: Mansion House or London Bridge)

Leadenhall Market is used throughout the films as Diagon Alley. The Glass House Opticians shop in Bull's Head Passage was used as the entrance to the Leaky Cauldron in *The Philosopher's Stone*. (Tube: Bank or Monument)

After crossing Lambeth Bridge, the Night Bus pulls up at **7 Stoney Street** in Borough and lets Harry off at the Leaky Cauldron. (Tube: London Bridge)

Scotland Yard is the location of the red telephone box in which Harry and Mr Weasley descend into the secret Ministry of Magic in *The Order of the Phoenix*. (Tube: St James's Park)

The public toilets in **Whitehall** were used as the entrance to the Ministry of Magic in *The Deathly Hallows*. (Tube: Westminster)

Australia House on the Strand served as Gringott's Bank. The marble interior is open during London Open House weekend (see page 13). (Tube: Temple or Covent Garden)

The Reptile House at **London Zoo** is where Harry first speaks parcel tongue in *The Philosopher's Stone*. (Tube: Camden Town)

Platform 9¾, from where the steam train departs to Hogwarts, is really Platform 4 at **King's Cross** station; look out for the plaque and for half a shopping trolley disappearing into the wall. The exterior of **St Pancras** station is the backdrop for the flying car sequence in *The Chamber of Secrets*. (Tube: King's Cross St Pancras)

Hermione's home in *The Deathly Hallows* is just off Hampstead Heath, on **Heathgate**, with St Jude the Martyr's church in the background. (Tube: Golders Green and bus H2)

Don't miss London Eye

County Hall, Westminster Bridge Rd SE1 7PB, T0871-781 3000, londoneye.com. 1-7 Jan daily 1000-1800, 22 Jan-Mar daily 1000-2000, Apr and Sep daily 1000-2100, May-Jun Sun-Thu 1000-2100, Fri-Sat 1000-2130, Jul-Aug daily 1000-2130, Oct-Dec daily 1000-2030, Christmas Eve 1000-1730, New Year's Eve 1000-1500, closed Christmas Day and 8-21 Jan. £18.90, £11.25 child (4-15), under 4s free, £53.60 family. Cheaper tickets available for 'flights' pre-booked online (up to 2 hrs before visit) at weekends and Jun-Sep. Tube: Westminster or Waterloo.

Officially opened on New Year's Eve 1999, the London Eye has quickly become one of the architectural icons of modern London, vying with the Houses of Parliament and Nelson's Column as a symbol of the city, and recognized from Hollywood to Bollywood. It has been rescued from collapse by the Fantastic Four, featured as a romantic backdrop to song and dance routines in *Namaste* and to courtships in the rom-com *Wimbledon*, and used as a viewing platform by the Simpsons searching for their wayward kids. A trip to London without a ride on the Eye has become almost as unthinkable as a visit to New York without a stint on top of the Empire State Building.

The wheel rotates sedately, lifting you 443 ft (135 m) above the Thames to make Parliament (and the crowds milling on the South Bank) miniature and, on a clear day, revealing a view over the capital that stretches as far south as the downs and north to the green and rolling hills beyond Hampstead and Muswell Hill. Viewing is from glass-sided pods, which move at around half a mile an hour. 'Flights' last 30 minutes and there is little risk of boredom; even the smallest children become transfixed with the views and the vastness of the 1700-ton structure, with its rope-like cables and massive spokes and arches. The process of getting on to the attraction, however, is painful. Expect to queue for well over an hour in the open air at weekends or during the peak summer season and to be shepherded like battery livestock by the curt and uninterested staff. Be sure to bring an umbrella and a friend to take the kids to the adjacent playground – which is free and which has slides, swings and climbing frames – while you brave the queues. (There are lavatories with nappy-changing facilities in the ticket office.)

Merlin Entertainments, which run the Eye, offer an extended range of packages, including sunset and night flights, together with multi-ticket discounts to their other attractions which include the adjacent Aquarium, nearby London Dungeon and Madame Tussaud's. The London Eye also has some ancillary attractions. These include a tiny and crowded **skating rink** (poor value compared to Somerset House and Streatham) and the **London Eye Cruise**, which runs a few hundred metres north to the Houses of Parliament before cruising east a little beyond Tower Bridge. Guide commentary is unimaginative and perfunctory and there are better-value boat tours (see page 22).

> **❝❞**
> It may take a while but my favourite thing in London is the London Eye. I like that you can see all that London has to offer. I feel like I'm in space so some dreams may come true.
>
> **Benji, aged eight**

Five viewpoints in central London

The Monument
Monument St, EC3R, T020-7626 2717, themonument.info. Daily 0930-1730 (last entry 1700), closed 24-26 Dec and 1 Jan. £3, £1 child. Tube: Monument or London Bridge.
Christopher Wren's homage in Portland stone to the Great Fire of 1666 has 311 tortuous steps leading to a burnished flaming orb housing a tiny gallery 202 ft (62 m) above London, with views over the river, City and Blackfriars.

St Paul's Cathedral (see page 76).

Tower Bridge Exhibition (see page 42).

Wellington Arch
Hyde Park Corner, W1J 7JZ, T020-7798 9055, english-heritage.org. uk. Apr-Oct Wed-Sun 1000-1700, Nov-Mar Wed-Sun 1000-1600. £3.70, £1.90 child. Tube: Hyde Park Corner.
Panoramas over Green, St James's and Hyde parks, the Houses of Parliament and, if you time it right, the Household Cavalry passing beneath on their way to and from the Changing of the Guard at Horse Guards Parade (Wed-Sun 1040-1140).

Westminster Cathedral Tower
42 Francis St, Westminster, SW1P 1QW, T020-7798 9055, westminstercathedral.org.uk. Mon-Fri 0930-1700, Sat-Sun 0930-1800. Free. Tube: Victoria. Three hundred and sixty-degree views over Westminster and Pimlico from a gallery in the 210-ft (64-m) tall tower of this beautiful faux-Byzantine cathedral.

Out & about South Bank & Southwark

Big days out

London Dungeon

28-34 Tooley St, SE1 2SZ, T020-7403 7221, the-dungeons.co.uk. Daily 1000-1700 or later. £23, £17 child (10% cheaper online), combination tickets available with other Merlin attractions, including the London Eye and Madame Tussaud's. Tube: London Bridge.

The London Dungeon is not for the squeamish or for children under eight. After the tedium of long and winding queues, kids enter a gloomy labyrinth

Tortured by Troopsmen

66 99

The London Dungeon has some really super rides that will rattle your teeth. It makes me feel quite spine tingled to think that hundreds of years ago people were actually hung there!

Elâ, aged 10

of mirrors and then a series of corridors and rooms under the railway arches. Here they encounter a historical gore-fest of fake blood, severed rubber limbs and festering sores, spiced up further with smoking dry ice, choreographed cackles and squeals and spooky rides, culminating in a simulated hanging. It's all very tongue in cheek and great fun, staged by deliciously hammy actors. The show is a pot pourri of almost 500 years of the capital's historic horrors, from the plague and Great Fire of 1666, through medieval torture to clumsy Victorian surgery, a close shave with Sweeney Todd and an eyewitness account of the Ripper murders given by a busty Whitechapel streetwalker covered in wonderfully over-the-top stage make-up.

Sea Life London Aquarium

County Hall, Westminster Bridge Rd, SE1 7PB, T0871-663 1678, visitsealife. com. Mon-Thu 1000-1800 (last entry 1700), Fri-Sun 1000-1900 (last entry 1800). £18, £12.50 child, under 3s free (10% cheaper booked online), combination tickets available with other Merlin attractions (including the adjacent London Eye). Tube: Waterloo or Westminster.

London's second-largest aquarium (the aquarium in London Zoo is bigger) showcases some 500 aquatic species of fish, crustacean, reptile, mollusc, bird and

Hit or miss?

The London Bridge Experience & Tombs
2-4 Tooley St, SE1 2PF, T0844-847 2287, thelondonbridgeexperience. com. Mon-Fri 1000-1700, Sat-Sun 1000-1800. £23, £17 concessions, £74 family, discounts online. Tube: London Bridge.

This two-fold attraction begins with a potted and pantomime horrible history of London told by a handful of hammy actors. It's followed by a scurry through spooky mock tombs, where visitors are assailed by actors dressed as corpses, ghost train jumps and starts and general Chamber of Horrors gore. Like the very similar London Dungeon, it's not an attraction for smaller children and many visitors find the price unreasonably high.

echinoderm from almost every freshwater and marine ecosystem in low-lit, modern, imaginatively themed galleries. Highlights for kids include the 40 sharks (from 12 different species, including large hammerheads and corgi-sized dogfish), some of which are viewed from a large walk-through tank; a rainforest room with dripping vines concealing dwarf crocodiles and tanks of red piranhas, and the touch tank, where children can get messy with rock-pool creatures and learn to pick up lobsters and crabs. Fact-finder trails and cards encourage children to go and

Who are you looking at?

explore the clearly labelled and well-displayed tanks on their own. The Aquarium supports and emphasizes conservation; interactive screens and displays offer information on themes like pollution and over-fishing.

Tate Modern

Bankside, SE1 9TG, T020-7887 8888, kids.tate.org.uk. Sun-Thu 1000-1800, Fri-Sat 1000-2200, closed 24-26 Dec. Free except for some temporary exhibitions. Tube: Southwark.
In 2000, the Bankside power station, a creation of Sir Giles Gilbert Scott (who also designed the red phone box), was transformed by Swiss architects

Herzog and de Meuron into one of Europe's foremost modern art galleries. Its imposing presence – a vast atrium flooded with light and stunning high-spec galleries, packed with the best of modern and contemporary art – make the gallery a must-see. And there is no need to worry about children getting bored. Tate Modern offers a range of free attractions and activities for families. These include a bright red family zone on the Level 3 concourse with kids' art books and games, a multimedia guide to lead kids through the galleries and a more traditional paper trail aimed at helping kids look and learn about

London's best
spooky attractions

British Museum sleepover (see page 73).

Clink Prison Museum (see page 39).

Ham House (see page 128).

London Bridge Experience & Tombs (see page 36).

London Dungeon (see page 36).

Madame Tussaud's (see page 97).

Sir John Soane's Museum candlelight tour (see page 72).

Tower of London (see page 80).

Wellcome Collection (see page 41).

Tate Modern.

modern art. Both are available free from the Information Desks on Levels 1 and 2.

Art gluttons can catch the Tate to Tate boat outside the gallery (every 40 mins, £5, £2.50 child, under 5s free) from Tate Modern west along the river to **Tate Britain** (Millbank, SW1P 4RG, daily 1000-1800, 1000-2200 on the last Fri of the month, closed 24-26 Dec, free, tube: Pimlico), which showcases British art since the 1500s, from Elizabethan portraiture to the Turner Prize.

More family favourites

Britain at War Experience
64-66 Tooley St, SE1 2TF, T020-7403 3171, britainatwar.co.uk. Nov-Mar daily 1000-1630, Apr-Oct daily 1000-1700, closed 24-26 Dec. £12.95, £5.50 child, free under 5s. Tube: London Bridge.

This museum, which is not suitable for under 5s, allows visitors to experience life during the London Blitz. Displays, models of 1940s buildings and artefacts are mixed with state-of-the-art special sound and visual effects, which simulate the eerie buzz of a doodlebug, the explosions of the bombs and even the death and destruction they caused, with models of dead people and flying dust. Kids can dress up in tin helmets and gas masks and measure out rations.

Clink Prison Museum

Clink St, SE1 9DG, T020-7403 0900, clink.co.uk. Jul-Sep daily 1000-2100, Oct-Jun Mon-Fri 1000-1800, Sat-Sun 1000-1930, closed Christmas Day. £6, £5.50 child (prices include a photo). Tube: London Bridge.

While the London Dungeon offers gore with a garnish of education, the Clink Prison Museum offers education with a garnish of gore. The museum is a recreation of the genuine Clink Prison, one of the city's first, dating from 1144 and used to incarcerate both adults and children. Tours focus not only on the jail itself but the surrounding area: a maze of alleys and arcades on the south bank of the Thames owned by the Bishop of Winchester and home to bull- and bear-baiting pits, theatres (including the Globe) and a notorious red-light district whose workers were known as 'Winchester Geese'. The prison is said to be one of the most haunted locations in London.

Design Museum

28 Shad Thames, SE1 2YD, T0870-833 9955, designmuseum.org. Daily 1000-1745. £8.50, £5 concessions, under 12s free. Tube: London Bridge or Tower Hill.

Exhibits include everything from mass-produced objects like the Philippe Starck Berta kettle to the Sinclair C5 and motorway signs. Most are displayed in temporary exhibitions. The museum has one of the most extensive children's activity programmes of any in the city, with explorer trails throughout the museum, workshops and family days (see page 43).

Film Museum

County Hall, Westminster Bridge Rd, SE1 7PB, T020-7202 7040, londonfilmmuseum.com. Mon-Fri 1000-1700, Sat 1000-1800, Sun 1100-1800. £13.50, £11.50 concessions, £9.50 child, under 5s free. Tube: Waterloo or Westminster.

Costumes, sets, props and memorabilia from many of the hundreds of films made in Britain since the 1950s are showcased in this 2800-sq m emporium housed in the former headquarters of the Greater London Council. There are items on display from the *Harry Potter*, *Indiana Jones*, *Superman*, *Batman*, *Alien* and *Star Wars* series, alongside one-offs like *Sherlock Holmes*, *Clash of the Titans* and *The Green*

Zone. Look out for costumes from *Alien*, *Excalibur* and *Harry Potter* by Terry English, iconic memorabilia, such as the original Rank Organisation gong, and temporary exhibitions, which, in the past, have covered everything from Ray Harryhausen's fabulous stop-motion creatures to Charlie Chaplin: the Great Londoner.

Golden Hinde

St Mary Overie Dock, 1 & 2 Pickfords Wharf, Clink St, SE1 9DG, T020-7403 0123, goldenhinde.com. Daily 1000-1730. £6, £4.50 child, family tickets available, higher prices for guided tours and fun days. Tube: London Bridge.

In 1577, 11 years before he defeated the Spanish Armada,

Out & about South Bank & Southwark

Sir Francis Drake became one of the first sailors to circumnavigate the world in a modest-looking wooden galleon, a replica of which is moored in a little dock near Shakespeare's Globe. En route he became the first European to set foot in California, naming it Nova Albion, and stole one of the largest hoards of treasure ever taken from the Spanish – enough to pay off the English national debt in one fell swoop. After Drake's return, his ship became so famous that it was put on public display on the south bank of the Thames – the earliest recorded example of a ship being preserved for public posterity. The original has long rotted away and the ship you see today is a full-size replica built in 1973 and staffed by actors dressed as Elizabethans; but it's also been round the globe, sailing a total of over 140,000 miles, many more than the original. The *Golden Hinde* is open daily for self-guided tours but the best way for children to see the ship is on one of the activity days (see page 43).

HMS Belfast

Morgan's Lane, Tooley St, SE1 2JH, T020-7940 6300, hmsbelfast.iwm. org.uk. Mar-Oct daily 1000-1800, Nov-Feb daily 1000-1700, closed 24-26 Dec. £12.95, under 16s free. Tube: London Bridge or Monument. Kids who love boats or big guns will adore this magnificent steel cruiser moored next to Tower Bridge. It is the only surviving vessel of its kind to have seen active service in World War II, during which time it was one of the largest ships in the Royal Navy. Belfast helped to sink the massive German warship, *Scharnhorst*, in the battle of the North Cape in 1943 and served until after the Korean War. It remains a formidable sight: 614 ft (187 m) long, 11,553 tons in weight and armed with 32 Bofors AA guns, the largest of which have six-inch barrels.

London Fire Brigade Museum

169 Union St, SE1 0EG, T020-8555 1200 ext 39894, london-fire.gov.uk. Visits by appointment only (via the phone or by emailing museum@ london-fire.gov.uk). £3, £1 child, under 6s free. Tube: Southwark. This handsome Georgian terraced house near Southwark Bridge was both the home and workplace for London's chief fire officers from 1878 to 1937. It's now a museum with a large collection of shiny historical engines, fire-fighting equipment and memorabilia illustrating the history of fire-fighting in London from the Great Fire of 1666 to the present.

Shakespeare's Globe

21 New Globe Walk, Bankside, SE1 9DT, T020-7902 1400, shakespeares-globe.org. Exhibition and tours Dec-Mar daily 1000-1730, Apr-Nov (theatre season) Mon-Sat 0900-1230 (Globe Theatre), 1300-1700 (Rose Theatre), Sun 0900-1130 (Globe Theatre), 1200-1700 (Rose Theatre). Tickets £5-35, tours £11.50, £7 child 5-15, under 5s free. Tube: Southwark or Mansion House.

The Globe is, of course, not Shakespeare's at all; it is a recreation of the medieval theatre used by the bard for the first

Take your medicine

Budding doctors and nurses might be intrigued by the **Old Operating Theatre Museum & Herb Garrett** (9a St Thomas's St, SE1 9RY, thegarret.org.uk, daily 1030-1700, £5.80, £3.25 child, tube: London Bridge), the oldest operating theatre in Europe, which is set in the timber-framed roof space of the 18th-century church of St Thomas, together with a reconstructed herbal apothecary. Both have been used for film sets. Further west, in St Thomas's, the great teaching hospital on the south bank of the Thames, is the **Florence Nightingale Museum** (St Thomas's Hospital, Lambeth Palace Rd, SE1 7EH, T020-7620 0374, florence-nightingale.co.uk, daily 1000-1700, closed Good Friday and 25-26 Dec, £5.80, £4.80 child including an audio tour, tube: Westminster or Waterloo). It houses exhibits and information telling the life story of the great Crimean War nurse and her Jamaican co-worker, Mary Seacole. There are also Victorian medical instruments, bric-a-brac from the war itself and Florence's pet owl, Athena, stuffed for posterity. Over 12s with morbid inclinations might want to visit the **Wellcome Collection** (183 Euston Rd, NW1 2BE, T020-7611 2222, wellcomecollection.org, Tue-Wed and Fri-Sun 1000-1800, Thu 1000-2200, free, tube: Euston), which charts the gruesome history of medicine in Britain through exhibits that include a torture chair, body parts and pictures of the pustulate and disease-ridden. Less grisly is the Wellcome Wing of the **Science Museum** (see page 61). The **Chelsea Physic Garden** (66 Royal Hospital Rd, SW3 4HS, T020-7352 5646, chelseaphysicgarden.co.uk, Apr-Oct Wed-Fri 1200-1700, Sun 1200-1700, £8, £5 child, under 5s free) is London's oldest botanic garden and was founded in the late 17th century as a place for apprentice pharmacists to learn about the medicinal qualities of plants. The garden preserves 5000 species, some of which are poisonous (and should not be touched). There are carnivorous sundews, mandrakes, aromatic herbs (used in the preparation of essential oils), anti-cancer plants like Madagascar periwinkle, woolly foxglove (used in the treatment of heart attack), and meadowsweet, the plant from which salicylic acid was first made in 1835, leading to the production of aspirin. There's also a pond, well stocked with non-bloodsucking leeches, water boatmen, dragonfly nymphs and other small invertebrates. The garden runs family activity days in season.

> 66 99
>
> I like going to Shakespeare's Globe because you can look at everything and learn about Elizabethan dress and about how much it cost to get into a play. I makes me feel like a real Elizabethan.
>
> **Geraldine, aged eight**

performances of many of his most famous plays, including *Romeo and Juliet*, *King Lear* and *Othello*. The original Globe lay a hundred metres or so away from the current waterfront site; it was partially destroyed in a fire in 1613 and demolished during the Civil War. The current edifice was the pet project of American actor turned Londoner, Sam Wanamaker. It is remarkably true to the Elizabethan original: a thatched roof shelters the stage and seating area, while the rest of the auditorium is open to the elements; the enormous stage is flanked by oak pillars supporting a canopy, and the actors wear period costume for performances. The spectacle and sense of historical context make this perhaps the best location in Britain to introduce an older child to Renaissance Theatre. Performances take place over the summer and are mostly works of Shakespeare, with a smattering of plays by his contemporaries, such as Marlowe, and the occasional new work. There is also an exhibition dedicated to Elizabethan theatre (open throughout the year) and

Top: The Golden Hinde.
Left: HMS Belfast.

guided tours of the theatre by Globe actors. (Note that during performances, the tours visit the excavations of the nearby Rose Theatre instead.)

Tower Bridge

206-208 Tower Bridge Rd, SE1 2UP, T020-7403 3761, towerbridge.org. uk. Apr-Sep daily 1000-1830, Oct Mar daily 0930-1800, closed 24-26 Dec and until 1200 on 1 Jan. £7, £3 child, under 5s free. Tube: Tower Hill.

It has since come to symbolize a pop-historical London of Sherlock Holmes and thick fogs, but when it was completed in 1894, Tower Bridge was a statement to the world of London's long-standing economic and technological might: an engineering feat that astonished the world. Its architectural style is rooted in tradition – complementing the Tower of London (see page 80), which sits next to the bridge on the north bank of the Thames – but its workings were state of the art, as a tour inside the bridge attests. Giant hydraulic engines powered by pressurized water from the Thames move the twin arms (or bascules), each of which weighs 1000 tons and which are pivoted on 70,000-ton concrete towers faced with stately Portland stone. They are so perfectly balanced that the bridge can be raised in less than five minutes. When the bridge was completed by George Stevenson, it was the largest and most sophisticated bascule bridge ever constructed, and probably the most expensive, costing the modern-day equivalent of £100 million. The bridge exhibition is worth visiting both for a glimpse of how the bridge works and for the wonderful views of London from the walkways which sit 213 ft (65 m) above the river.

Activity days & workshops

The **Golden Hinde** runs at least 21 days of organized activities every month and more during the summer, including guided historical tours, all-day living history encounters and pirate fun days (when kids have the chance to dress up as pirates, participate in a series of re-enactments and generally run riot on the boat). There are usually monthly sleepovers too for children between five and 10 years old (accompanied by an adult), which include an afternoon and evening of costumed activities, a Tudor dinner and sleeping out on the gun deck amongst the cannons. A Tudor breakfast of bread and cheese is provided in the morning, followed by a snack of hot chocolate.

The **Film Museum** (see page 39) has regular free workshops for kids, and competitions to win tickets to film premieres in Leicester Square. The **Southbank Centre** (see page 32) has numerous activities for kids. Type 'children' into the website search engine (southbankcentre.co.uk) at any time to reveal an eclectic spread of drop-in events (some of which are free), including dance, painting, poetry, jazz for juniors, classical concerts especially for children, plays and even gamelan workshops. **Shakespeare's Globe** (see page 40) works with children

Music workshops hit the right note.

Globe Theatre.

through an annual programme of Lively Action workshops, lectures and theatre encounter tours (globe-education.org). The **Design Museum** (see page 39) runs Get Creative workshops for budding designers aged five to 11 and their parents on Sundays (book ahead on T020-7940 8783, designmuseum.org, £8.50, £4

child). All are led by leading designers. They also have design family days and run an annual design competition for 10 to 14 year olds. Details are on the website. **Tate Modern** and **Tate Britain** (see pages 37 and 38) run occasional workshops for children and young people (kids.tate.org.uk).

Out & about Westminster

A visit to Westminster is a unique and very British experience. There is simply nowhere else on Earth where history, tradition and modern political power fuse together so potently and so openly. Children are welcome to wander through the corridors of power in the Houses of Parliament, up the tower to Big Ben and beyond the heavily policed gates at No 10 Downing Street. They can even walk through the Queen's home (when she's away in Scotland on holiday) and smell the roses in her garden. There are more attractions besides: a cluster of magnificent parks, museums and galleries, the city's most famous shopping streets and the West End, where London's theatres show new productions and popular, long-running musicals.

Fun & free

Watch the Changing of the Guard

The Queen's Guard in London comprises two detachments, one each for Buckingham Palace and St James's Palace, under the command of the Captain of the Queen's Guard. Every morning in summer or every other morning for the rest of the year at a prompt 1028 (0928 on a Sunday), ceremonial guardsmen, clad in scarlet coats with sparkling buttons and tall, furry, black

bearskin hats, and horsemen in shiny steel helmets topped with silk fronds, leave Hyde Park Barracks for Buckingham and St James's palaces. When they arrive they take 40 minutes to perform the Changing of the Guard ceremony, one of London's most famous daily displays of pomp and pageantry. You should turn up at Hyde Park Barracks (Knightsbridge, SW7, T020-7414 2574, tube: Knightsbridge) at 1020 to follow the soldiers on their march or arrive at either Buckingham Palace (tube: Hyde Park Corner, Victoria or Green Park) or St James's Palace (tube: Green Park) at 1130 to see the show.

During the day guards can also be seen outside the Household Cavalry Museum on Whitehall (see page 55), maintaining an absolutely stationary guard that is changed with similarly stiff but fun and free pageantry at 1100 every morning and 1000 on Sundays.

Hang out with Nelson & the lions

Trafalgar Square (tube: Charing Cross), London's largest square, is watched over by Admiral Nelson, who stands 184 ft (56 m) above the city on his famous column, surrounded by stately buildings. These include the **National Gallery** (see page 50), South Africa House and **St-Martin-in-the-Fields** (stmartin-in-the-fields.org), which has afternoon concerts with programmes for kids, many

of which are free. The city often hosts free events in the square. It is a favourite London meeting spot and a good place to loiter in the summer sunshine for a while. Children love to clamber over the huge black stone lions that sit at the base of Nelson's Column. Don't miss the **fourth plinth** in the northwest corner, which, after being empty for many years, is now used for specially commissioned and often intriguing artworks.

Do some royal birdwatching

From Trafalgar Square, **The Mall** leads west through **Admiralty Arch** to **Buckingham Palace** (see page 46). The road is used as a ceremonial route on special royal occasions and is coloured to resemble a red carpet leading up to the palace. It is flanked by **St James's Park** (tube: St James's Park) on the south side and **Green Park** (tube: Green Park) on the north, two of central London's most attractive green spaces. Their stately arcades of handsome trees, manicured lawns and ornamental ponds are a great place to stroll, have a picnic or let off steam, and belie the kind of scrofulous past adored by fans of 'horrible histories'. In the Middle Ages St James's was a leper colony and, then, the site of a

notorious brothel (masquerading as a convent), while Green Park was a leper's burial ground. Henry VIII cleaned up the bordellos, drained the marshland nearby and built St James's Palace, filling both parks with deer and using them as personal hunting grounds. In the Renaissance period, the parks regained their tawdry reputations, and were notorious for the prevalence of bawdy women and duels. They became elegant only when George IV commissioned John Nash to give central London its Regency facelift and to remodel nearby Buckingham Palace.

Today, both parks are great spots for urban birdwatching. The lake and its islands in St James's are home to colonies of

Out & about Westminster

breeding waterfowl, including mandarin, tufted and mallard ducks; barnacle, greylag, Canada, bar-headed and red-breasted geese, shelduck, black swans and pelicans. The last of these are fed by wildlife officers daily between 1430 and 1500 at Duck Island Cottage (marked on the park map). The parks' woodlands, meanwhile, are home to long-tailed tit, blue tit, great tit, robin, blackbird, wren, great spotted woodpecker and tawny owl, all of which breed here.

Window shop in the West End

If you've had your fill of Westminster's pomp and circumstance, take an urban stroll through the bright lights of central London. **Piccadilly Circus**, with its famous flashing neon signs is a good spot to start. Look out for the Shaftesbury memorial fountain topped by a statue of an archer, popularly known as Eros. The square is home to the London branch of **Ripley's Believe it or Not** (1 Piccadilly Circus, WIJ 0DA, T020-7238 0222, ripleyslondon.com, daily 1000-2230, £22, £18 child, under 4s free), an overpriced five-floor miscellany of curious objects and attractions, from two-headed calves to a dizzying 'topsy turvy tunnel'. Try to steer your teens away from the much advertised **Trocadero Centre** (7-14 Coventry St, W1D 7DH, trocadero.com), a giant games arcade designed to lure children in with a

bowling alley and state-of-the-art cinema screens. **Regent's Street**, a magnificent sweep of Regency buildings designed by Nash, leaves Piccadilly from the northwestern corner, leading past the self-proclaimed 'best toyshop in the world', **Hamleys** (see page 176), to **Oxford Circus** and **Oxford Street**, the busiest shopping street in the city. East of Regent Street is **Soho**, whose once-notorious streets are full of cafés, shops, music venues and pubs and are busy with people at all times of the day and night. Leave Soho to the southeast to reach **Leicester Square**, London's cinema central, surrounded on four sides by expensive big-screen multiplexes that host movie premieres (just off the square the Prince Charles cinema, princecharlescinema.com, is one of the cheapest in London). Next to Leicester Square is **Chinatown**, whose cheap restaurants (some

more wholesome and authentic than others) are a great place to re-fuel after pounding the pavements.

Big days out

Buckingham Palace

Buckingham Palace Rd, London SW1A 1AA, T020-7766 7300, royalcollection.org.uk. Summer only daily 0900-1730 (last entry 1630). Royal Day Out £31, £17.50 under 17s, £81.50 family. State Rooms only £17.50, £10 under 17s, £46 family, under 5s free. Guided tours from £65. Tube: Green Park, St James's Park or Victoria.

The palace, originally the Duke of Buckingham's house, was bought in 1761 by George III for his wife Queen Charlotte as a family home close to the official royal residence of St James's Palace. George IV decided that the building should become his home and commissioned

Nash to remodel it as a palace. The architect doubled the building's size, demolished most of the original and rebuilt it in the French neoclassical style that had earned him favour with the prince. He added a massive triumphal arch, the Marble Arch, as the centrepiece of an enlarged courtyard to commemorate the British victories over Napoleon at Trafalgar and Waterloo. But designs and execution became so costly and delayed that the king never moved in to Buckingham Palace and Nash lost his job. After George's death, William IV commissioned Edmund Blore to complete the palace, then offering the building as a new parliament after the Palace of Westminster burnt down in 1834. The building finally became a royal residence under Queen

Out & about Westminster

Victoria who moved in with her beloved Albert three weeks after her accession in 1837. The queen found the palace too small for her family, moved the Marble Arch to the north of Hyde Park (where it sits rather incongruously to this day) and added a fourth wing. The cost of the new wing was largely covered by the sale of George IV's Royal Pavilion at Brighton (see page 160).

The palace is open to visitors during the summer only, when the 'Royal Day Out' ticket (available by queuing at the palace door or in advance online) gives access to the State Rooms, the Royal Mews and the Queen's Gallery. The State Rooms (open during the Queen's annual visit to Scotland, usually Aug-Sep) are used by the Queen to receive official guests, and include a lavish banqueting hall and a throne room. The rooms are decorated with priceless paintings by Rembrandt, Rubens, Poussin and Canaletto, sculpture by Canova, Sèvres porcelain and exquisite English and French gilt furniture. The mews are the queen's working stables, where visitors can see Her Majesty's Cleveland Bay (a uniquely British breed of carriage horse), the Windsor grey horses and the Gold State Coach, last used during the Queen's Golden Jubilee in 2002 to carry Her Majesty and Prince Philip to St Paul's Cathedral, and rumoured

National Gallery.

to be the carriage which will be used for William's marriage to Kate Middleton. The **Queen's Gallery** (daily 1000-1730, last admission 1630, £9 adult, £4.50 child) is a permanent exhibition space showing a rotating display of items from the Royal Collection, which includes one of the most extensive assemblages of old masters in the world, alongside treasures such as Chinese porcelain, Fabergé eggs and jewellery. Details of current exhibitions can be found on the website. If the velvet ropes, pomp and paintings all get too much for young children, there is a nature trail in the palace gardens and a drop-in

family space, where guides host activities for children from six to 11 years old.

National Gallery

Trafalgar Sq, WC2N 5DN, T020-7747 2885, nationalgallery.org.uk. Sat-Thu 1000-1800, Fri 1000-2100. Free. Tube: Charing Cross or Leicester Square. Britain's foremost art gallery has a collection of Western European art to rival any of the great museums of Europe and, unlike the Louvre, the Uffizi or the Prado, it doesn't charge an entrance fee. There are masterpieces from every major European school of painting from the 13th to the 19th centuries and, with

2300 canvases by the likes of Leonardo, Michelangelo, van Eyck, Rembrandt, Caravaggio and Monet, there will be something to enthral even the most restless of children. The gallery is spacious, bright, clearly laid out and offers a choice of self-guided audio tours. The gallery's 'ArtStart interactive guide' is a good way of introducing interested older children to the collection. Interactive multimedia screens profile 30 of the most popular paintings as a prelude to seeing the actual canvases. They are organized under a series of themes, which include 'Drunkenness and Debauchery' and 'Impressionism'. The ArtStart room is in the Sainsbury Wing; there are a further 14 screens in the East Wing espresso bar and multimedia room, where parents and children can browse the collection at their leisure over a juice or a coffee (all the restaurants and cafés have kids' menus). There's also an online gallery of children's artwork inspired by the collection.

Palace of Westminster
Parliament Sq, SW1A 0AA, T020-7219 3000, parliament.uk/visiting. UK residents can arrange a free tour of the Palace and/or Clock Tower through their MP. Paid guided tours for all visitors are available Aug-Sep during summer opening (exact dates on the website) and Oct-Jul Sat 0915-1630. From £12, under 5s

Visiting Downing Street

Children can step inside the gates of Downing Street to watch ministers go to and fro through the doors of No 10 and No 11 but only as part of an organized excursion arranged through a school or club. Write to the Direct Communications Unit at either the Home Office (2 Marsham St, SW1P 4DF, T020-7035 4848, 0900-1700 Mon-Fri) or Downing Street (T020-7807 3079) to check availability. A formal request is then required by post or fax (F020-7925 0918) and should include the names of all the adults wishing to visit and the number of children. Downing Street can reply to your office or send a confirmation letter directly to the group if you include the address.

free. Book in advance or prepare to queue. Tube: Westminster.
Although most of the current building dates from the 19th century, the Palace of Westminster has been a seat of London power since William Rufus constructed Westminster Hall on marshland in the 11th century. The Palace of Westminster was the London residence of English monarchs until a fire in 1512 forced Henry VIII to relocate to the Palace of Whitehall. Westminster became the permanent seat of parliament, while Whitehall remained the main royal residence in London until 1698, when it too was almost entirely destroyed by a fire. The Palace of Whitehall was larger than both the Vatican and Versailles but today only Inigo Jones's **Banqueting House** (Whitehall at Horse Guards Av, hrp.org.uk, £4.80, free under 18s) remains.

In 1834 another fire at Westminster destroyed all but Westminster Hall, the Cloisters of St Stephen's, the Chapel of St Mary Undercroft and the Jewel Tower. The Palace of Westminster was once again built anew on an even grander scale. Charles Barry (who planned the overall design) and Augustus Pugin (who added the

Westminster in children's fiction

In the *Bartimaeus* trilogy by Jonathan Stroud, the British government is run by magicians and Parliament is assailed and attacked by demons. There are fast-paced, adrenalin-rushing scenes in Parliament, Westminster Abbey and Whitehall.

In *Harry Potter and the Half Blood Prince* by JK Rowling, Cornelius Fudge, Minister for Magic, negotiates with a muggle (non-wizard) prime minister, who bears a resemblance to John Major, and Death Eaters ransack the South Bank.

Adrian's long-term sweetheart Pandora becomes a minister in the Blair government in *Adrian Mole and the Weapons of Mass Destruction* by Sue Townsend.

A band of orphan children led by the irrepressible Dido Twite foil a plot to destroy Parliament in *Black Hearts in Battersea* by John Aiken, set in an alternative 19th-century London.

Scorpia by Anthony Horowitz is an edge-of-your-seat action adventure set in London, in which a 14-year-old secret agent recruited by MI6 visits Parliament to consult with the British prime minister in order to avert a plot to murder teenaged children and the English reserve football team.

decoration and detail) built a statement in stone of Britain's wealth and confidence at the height of its imperial power, capping their Gothic revival masterpiece with a monumental 315-ft (96-m) tall clock tower, which has come to be known after its 16-ton iron bell, **Big Ben**.

The clamber up the 393 vertiginous stairs of the **Westminster Clock Tower** is literally breathtaking. Big Ben itself has a crack in its side and is inscribed with the name of the Chief Commissioner of Works, Benjamin Hall, who oversaw the engineering and construction of the building. Big Ben is thought to be named either after him, or after a famously fat Westminster pub owner and amateur boxer, Benjamin Caunt. The bell sits in a belfry together with a number of quarter bells. Their collective chimes play a melody loosely based on Handel's 'I know that my redeemer liveth'. The

clock remains one of the most accurate mechanical timepieces in the world, failing only on a few occasions: once on New Year's Eve in 1862 because of heavy snow and ice; once in May 2005 because of 'unseasonable heat'; and once in August 1976, when the clock was shut down for a month of repairs after the 100-year-old Victorian winding drum wore out.

Members of the lower house began to convene in St Stephen's Chapel from 1550; the Victorian and entirely secular chambers of the modern **House of Commons** still retain many ecclesiastical accoutrements and a quasi-religious feel. Look out for the green pew-like benches and the Speaker's chair, which looks like a bishop's throne and sits in front of what looks remarkably like a sacristy. Although older children might be intrigued to see the prime minister or famous political figures familiar from TV, they will be bored rigid by most Commons debates, which are often conducted in a semi-deserted chamber and dominated by tedious points of order. Things get lively at noon each day during Question Time, however, when the air is alive with heckles, boos and cheers, and the debates are at their most colourful. On Wednesdays, Question Time is addressed to the Prime Minister. Free tickets should be requested in advance through a local MP to secure entrance for busy debates and for Prime Minister's Question Time. Overseas visitors and UK residents without tickets can queue outside the Cromwell Green visitor entrance but will only gain admission if there is space after ticket holders have entered. (Note that visiting children must be old enough to sign their name in the visitor's book, although babies and toddlers are not prohibited entry.) Tickets are not required at other periods but a wait of one or two hours is common. There's usually far less of a wait to view Parliament's other political chamber, the **House of Lords**, in action. This upper house may have less power but it is altogether grander and more spacious than the Commons.

The Palace of Westminster also retains a handful of its original medieval rooms. The grandest of these is **Westminster Hall**, the centrepiece of William Rufus's royal palace but embellished since, with a magnificent oak beam ceiling added in the 14th century. The hall was at one time England's supreme court of justice; Anne Boleyn, Thomas More and Charles I were condemned to death here and, in revenge for the latter, Oliver Cromwell's head was later impaled on the roof of the building by Royalists. It was also once used as a royal tennis court (16th-century balls were found jammed in the ceiling in the 1940s). The **Jewel Tower** (Abingdon St, SW1P 3JX, T020-7222 2219, english-heritage.org. uk, Mar-Oct daily 1000-1700, Nov-Feb daily 1000-1600, £3, £1.50 child) is another relic of the medieval palace, though a far less impressive one. The royal jewels are long gone and in their place is a small museum with a collection of royal bric-a-brac and a large and rather dull selection of weights and measures.

More family favourites

Churchill War Rooms
Clive Steps, King Charles St, SW1A 2AQ, T020-7930 6961, cwr.iwm.org. uk. Daily 0930-1800. £14.95, under 16s free. Tube: Westminster.

Winston Churchill, his cabinet ministers and some 500 civil servants planned and executed British military strategy during World War II in these extensive underground bunkers beneath Whitehall. The War Rooms included a hospital, sleeping quarters, a refectory and a rifle range, as well as the administrative offices. Only a small portion are open to the public. These include Churchill's office (converted from a broom cupboard) and bed chamber, and a series of rooms furnished and decorated as they were during the war, with heavy chintz armchairs, big Bakelite phones, cumbersome switchboards and maps

Rodin's Burghers of Calais in Victoria Tower Gardens.

showing half the world in British imperial red. All visitors are provided with a free personal audio guide, available in English (adult, child, family and visually impaired versions) and other languages. The gift shop stocks children's games.

Courtauld Gallery

Courtauld Institute of Art, Somerset House, Strand, WC2R 0RN, T020-7872 0220, courtauld.ac.uk. Daily 1000-1800, closed 25-26 Dec. £6, £4.50 concessions, child free, free to all Mon 1000-1400. Tube: Temple or Charing Cross.

This small gallery is a little-known London treasure, preserving the best collection of Impressionist and post-Impressionist art in Britain, and one of the finest outside France, as well as showing some of London's better temporary exhibitions. The collection was assembled by the millionaire American-born British industrialist Samuel Courtauld, who was one of the first collectors of French Impressionist paintings. The gallery has outstanding works charting the development of modern French painting from Monet and Renoir to Seurat and Gauguin. Masterpieces include van Gogh's *Self-Portrait with Bandaged Ear*, Manet's *A Bar at the Folies-Bergère*, Renoir's *La Loge* and works by Cézanne, including *Montagne Sainte Victoire*.

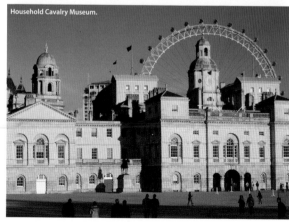

Household Cavalry Museum.

Household Cavalry Museum

Horse Guards, Whitehall, SW1A 2AX, T020-7930 3070, household cavalrymuseum.co.uk. Mar-Sep daily 1000-1800, Oct-Feb daily 1000-1700. £6.50, £4.50 child, under 4s free. Tube: Westminster or Embankment.

The museum displays miscellaneous military and civilian bric-a-brac, ranging from the cork leg which belonged to the Marquis of Anglesey – he lost his real one at Waterloo – to Jackie Charlton's football cap and lavish ceremonial uniforms, royal standards, medals, musical instruments and silverware by Fabergé. Most children are more interested in the working stables, where they can see the horses being fed, groomed and saddled before marching on parade with coats and freshly polished hooves shining. The museum also runs a variety of seasonal children's activities. These include trails around the museum with clues and a small prize for each correct entry, craft weekends (all with connections to the museum) and storytelling. All must be pre-booked.

National Portrait Gallery

St Martin's Place, WC2H 0HE, T020-7306 0055, npg.org.uk. Mon-Wed and Sat-Sun 1000-1800, Thu-Fri 1000-2100. Free. Charing Cross or Leicester Square.

The National Portrait Gallery offers a fascinating visual tour of Britain's political and cultural history through portraits of the great, the good, the not so good, the glitzy and the glamorous. The collection is half stately home stairway and half Madame Tussaud's, with aristocratic ancestors, such as Mary Queen of Scots and Admiral Nelson, sitting alongside contemporary cultural celebs like a muscled David Beckham, Paul Merton hugging a dolphin or a morose-looking indigo Lily Allen.

Royal Academy of Arts

Burlington House, Piccadilly, W1J 0BD, T020-7300 8000, royalacademy.org. uk. Sat-Thu 1000-1800, Fri 1000-1000. Permanent collection free, prices for exhibitions vary. Tube: Piccadilly.

The National Gallery may boast the finest collection of old master art in London but the Royal Academy hosts the best shows, including the famous 'Summer Exhibition' of emerging art from academy members, which has been held every year since 1769. Recent exhibitions have included the first major van Gogh exhibition in London for over 40 years, displaying over a hundred of van Gogh's paintings and drawings; a wonderful show of photographs of old London buildings, and 'How I See Myself', an exhibition showcasing the winners of the children's Junior Painter of the Year competition. There is also a permanent collection in the John Madejski Fine Rooms, with some wonderful paintings from hundreds of artists including children's favourites Constable, Turner and Spencer. The academy was founded by George III in 1768 and it remains a privately funded institution led by eminent artists whose purpose is 'to promote the creation, enjoyment and appreciation of the visual arts through exhibitions, education and debate'. John Constable, Thomas Gainsborough, JMW Turner and Stanley Spencer were all past members; current members include Norman Foster, Richard Rogers, David Hockney and Antony Gormley.

Statue of Joshua Reynolds outside the Royal Academy of Arts.

Out & about Westminster

Wallace Collection

Hertford House, Manchester Sq, W1U 3BN, T020-7563 9500, wallacecollection.org. Daily 1000-1700. Free. Tube: Bond Street.

This small but sumptuous collection of paintings, porcelain and furniture housed in a grand mansion just off London's shopping central, is a great spot to introduce kids to the likes of Hals, Rembrandt, Rubens, Poussin and Titian on a less overwhelming scale and in less overcrowded surroundings. The gallery is almost deserted on a winter weekday.

Westminster Abbey

20 Dean's Yard, SW1P 3PA, T020-7222 5152, westminster-abbey.org. Tube: Westminster.

No other building in England is as soaked in national history or as imposingly grand as this 1000-year-old temple to the English establishment. Pillars and arches soar to high ceilings in a series of magnificent chapels, and the nave, at over 115 ft (35 m) high is the tallest and perhaps the most magnificent in England. God and Christ barely get a look in, but every nook and cranny is crammed with tombs or memorials to dead prime ministers, kings, queens and English men and women of high renown. The pomp and grandeur are certainly awe-inspiring but they can also be overwhelming, especially for young children who easily tire of the clutter of

monuments and the endless crowded procession of shuffling tourist feet and perhaps yearn for a little space or time to soak in the atmosphere or sense of history. The best way to visit may be to imbue children with a sense of excitement over a particular tomb or sight before arriving. Jonathan Stroud's wonderful *Bartimaeus* trilogy (see box, page 52) features extensive spooky scenes in the abbey and serves as an excellent prelude to a visit for magic-minded 10-year-olds and above.

Highlights include the **Chapel of Edward the Confessor**, the resting place of the last king of Wessex and one of the last Saxon kings of England, parts of which date from the 13th century. English kings, including Henry II, Edward I, Edward III, Henry V and Richard II are buried nearby. More kings and queens are buried in and around the

This page: Westminster Abbey.
Opposite page: Ice skating at Somerset House.

fan-vaulted **Lady Chapel**, one of the greatest masterpieces of English medieval architecture. They include Henry VII, Elizabeth I, Charles II and George II. William Pitt, Gladstone and Palmerston are buried in the **North Transept**, known colloquially as 'Statesman's Aisle', and there are memorials to Disraeli and Sir Robert Peel, who founded the Metropolitan Police. Look out for the monument to Lady Elizabeth Nightingale, which features a figure of a skeletal Death emerging from a cave to aim an arrow at the heart of the dying lady. The **South Transept** is known as Poet's Corner. Chaucer, Edmund Spenser, Tennyson, Dickens, Dr Johnson, Kipling, Hardy, Garrick and Laurence Olivier lie here, alongside memorials to countless other writers. Shakespeare, who was originally buried in Stratford, was moved to Poet's Corner in 1740. Composers including Henry Purcell, Vaughan Williams and Herbert Howells are buried in the **Quire** and there are memorials to Sir Edward Elgar and Benjamin Britten. **Gardens** and vaulted **cloisters** surround the church. The latter lead to the exquisite octagonal **Chapter House**, where the King's Great Council of 1257 was first assembled, effectively marking the beginning of the English Parliament. In the vestibule of the Chapter House is the oldest door in Britain, dated to the 1050s. The **High Altar**, at

the sacred heart of the church, features a stunning 13th-century Italian mosaic made up of hundreds of shards of glass and semi-precious stones. There is a museum in the vaulted crypt, showing effigies of yet more kings and politicians.

Action stations

Activity days & workshops

The **National Gallery** (see page 50) has a mesmerizing range of activities for children, from audio tours and printed trails, holiday workshops and family Sundays to interactive story sessions for under fives. The **National Portrait Gallery** (see page 55) runs weekend and holiday workshops for children and toddlers; the full programme is on the website (npg.org.uk). Activities and workshops at the **Royal Academy of Arts** (see page 55) vary from month to month, but in the past they have

included 'exploring sculpture' (with an interactive slide show and talk, a visit to the exhibition and a practical hands-on session), 'art, fashion and identity' (exploring ideas of dress, fashion, identity and performing through hands-on activities and tours of the galleries) and free worksheets for young visitors. Most are free with an exhibition ticket, but pre-booking is essential.

Ice skating

In winter there's a temporary rink in the main courtyard of **Somerset House** (Strand, WC2R 1LA, T0844-844 2121, somersethouse.org.uk, daily 1000-1615. £10.50, £7.50 child, £30 family; tube: Charing Cross). It's the best one in central London and has two areas: one for more confident skaters and another with ice guides dressed as giant penguins to help smaller children. The guides must be booked in advance (£30).

Out & about Kensington, Chelsea & Knightsbridge

These celebrity-saturated boroughs have been fashionable since Sir Thomas More moved here in the 1520s, setting a trend for nobles from Henry VIII's court and eventually even enticing the king himself. The area was a favourite of William and Mary and of Queen Victoria, under whose reign the Natural History, Science and Victoria & Albert museums were constructed, and all of which remain fabulously popular with children. Diana Princess of Wales lived in Kensington Palace at the far end of one of the area's many beautiful parks, all of which are welcome acres of green space for kids weary of urban London.

Fun & free

Park & ride

Hyde Park (royalparks.gov.uk, tube: Hyde Park Corner) and the adjacent **Kensington Gardens** (see page 60) together comprise the largest green space in central London. Hyde Park was taken by Henry VIII from the monks of Westminster Abbey after the dissolution of the monasteries. Under the monks it had been semi-wild country but Henry turned it into a deer park and a private hunting ground, which it largely remained until the reign of Charles I who opened it to the general public. The park became a famous hang-out for brigands in the 17th century, so much so that when William III moved his court to Kensington Palace he found the route to St James's so dangerous that he had a personal highway constructed, lit with 300 oil lamps, thus creating the first artificially lit road in Britain. The Route de Roi survives today on the south side of the park, anglicized as **Rotten Row**. After George II was mugged in the park, losing the buckles of his shoes, his wallet and watch, his wife Queen Caroline had extensive renovations carried out which included adding an artificial lake, the **Serpentine**, made by damming the underground River Westbourne. But the park remained tawdry and was the capital's most popular duelling ground in the

18th and early 19th centuries. By the reign of the George IV it had also increasingly become an arena for public celebrations, including fireworks to celebrate the end of the Napoleonic Wars, and, in 1851, Queen Victoria staged the Great Exhibition here. During the 20th century, the park became famous as a venue for large-scale pop and rock concerts, including the Rolling Stones' now-legendary free concert in 1971, which attracted 80,000 fans; nearly double that number turned up for the Live 8 benefit concert in 2005. The park remains a venue for big public events, with a concert or two almost every summer and a Winter Fair in December. For the **2012 London Olympics**, the park will host the triathlon and the 10-km open water swimming events.

Hyde Park is a delight to walk around with children. Large lawned stretches mix with long avenues of stately London plane trees, formal rose gardens and little coppices. There is a playground, a number of cafés for tea, cakes and ice cream and plenty of grassy knolls and shady areas for a picnic (buy provisions in supermarkets in nearby Knightsbridge, Kensington or Bayswater).

The **Serpentine** remains the park's defining feature, famous for its lido (see page 68) and overlooked by an excellent café. On the north side of the Serpentine is the **Diana Princess of Wales memorial fountain**, opened by the Queen on 6 July 2004. It's a sinuous two-tier stream flowing over 545 pieces of perfectly sculpted Cornish granite descending through champagne-like bubbles into a calm pool, which you can dip your toes into. It receives around one million visitors each year. Other attractions include three children's playgrounds at the lido, tennis centre and near

Out & about Kensington, Chelsea & Knightsbridge

Edinburgh Gate. For more on sports in the park, see page 68.

Hyde Park is surrounded by minor monuments. At Hyde Park Corner, on the park's south-eastern edge, the **Wellington Arch** sits at the centre of one of the city's biggest and busiest roundabouts. The arch was originally crowned with a monumental statue of the Duke of Wellington mounted on his horse, Copenhagen, but the statue was so unpopular that it was replaced in 1912 with the current assemblage of horses pulling a chariot of

> **66 99**
> I love walking along the Serpentine in Hyde Park at dusk. You can see loads of bats, ducks and once I saw eight herons all walking on the grass.
>
> **Kiera, aged 12**

peace. A different and more refined statue of Wellington astride Copenhagen sits nearby. There are views out over the city from balconies on the arch (see page 35). Immediately opposite Wellington Arch is the Duke's former London abode, **Apsley House** (149 Piccadilly, W1J 7NT, T020-7499 5676, english-heritage.org.uk, Apr-Oct daily 1000-1700, Nov-Mar Wed-Sun 1000-1600, £4, £2 child). It was built in 1771 for the former Lord Chancellor, Baron Apsley and was originally known as 'Number One, London'. Inside is a beautiful, sweeping semi-circular staircase, a statue of a naked, heroic Napoleon – bought by Wellington, presumably for him to gloat at – and a small museum with an exhibit devoted to the Wellington boot. At the northeastern corner of the park and the far end of

Oxford Street is **Marble Arch**, moved here from Buckingham Palace by Victoria and looking lost in another sea of traffic. There's also a wonderful, colossal bronze cast of a horse's head here, by British sculptor Nic Fiddian-Green, which is a real favourite with children. A hundred metres south of Marble Arch is **Speaker's Corner**, which has been given over to the soapbox orator every Sunday for more than a century. Anyone can speak or demonstrate here on any subject without police permission. Come to hear everything from hellfire sermons and denunciations of the Gulf War to political diatribes and prophetic proclamations of the imminent arrival of extra-terrestrials. In the south of the park at the top of Exhibition Road is the **Albert Memorial**, an unsightly neo-Gothic spire by George Gilbert Scott, built to mark Prince Albert's untimely death in 1862. You can see his likeness beneath the turret, reading a catalogue from the Great Exhibition.

Never grow up

Kensington Gardens is contiguous with Hyde Park, immediately to the west. It was part of the park until William III bought it in 1689 as a front lawn for Kensington Palace, which overlooks it behind high wooden fences to the west. The ordered gardens, with

their flower beds, walkways and fountains, contrast with quasi-wild Hyde Park and are equally pleasant for a stroll or picnic. Look out for the statue of **Peter Pan** by George Frampton, with the boy who never grew up standing on a pedestal covered with climbing squirrels, rabbits and mice. He was sculpted long before Disney re-designed his appearance. The gardens are home to the **Serpentine Gallery** (T020-7402 6075, serpentinegallery.org, daily 1000-1800, closed 24-26 Dec and 1 Jan, free) although children might be more thrilled by the best playground in central London, the **Diana Memorial Playground** (Feb and late Oct 1000-1645, Mar and early Oct 1000-1745, Apr and Sep 1000-1845, May-Aug 1000-1945, Nov-Jan 1000-1545, free). The centrepiece is a half-scale wooden pirate ship, complete with climbing

frame masts and rope walkways, set in a sandy beach. Nature trails lead from the ship into semi-wooded areas, to teepees and other areas with various toys and play sculptures. There's plenty of seating so the grown-ups can relax too. The playground café serves salads, sandwiches, snacks, ice creams, juices and canned drinks, and has a children's menu. There are also toilets, with disabled and nappy-changing facilities. Elsewhere in the gardens is an **allotment**, where children can learn about growing their own food and tending small farm animals. There are also deck chairs for hire and a number of excellent cafés and refreshment points, the best of which is the **Broadwalk Café**.

Go car-spotting in Knightsbridge

London's Vanity Fair is played out less than a mile east of South Kensington in Knightsbridge, where every summer multi-millionaires from the Gulf States and their designer-clad girlfriends flout parking laws outside the Ladurée Macaroon café in Harrods, with their multi-million-pound 253-mph Bugatti Veyrons, Koenigsegg CCXRs and Lamborghini Murcielagos. Matt Master of *Top Gear* magazine commented in August 2010 that: "London is now the supercar capital", ahead of Monaco or Monte Carlo, and

it's a great spot for a wander with sports car-obsessed kids. The streets of Knightsbridge are also home to numerous little cafés, like **Paul** (see page 185), perfect for a cake pit stop after hours in the Exhibition Road museums. And, of course, there's **Harrods**, the celebrity-visited super-department store, which allegedly sells anything and everything at a price, and its more discreet and perhaps more tasteful rival nearby, **Harvey Nicholls**.

Big days out

Science Museum
Exhibition Rd, South Kensington SW7 2DD, T0870-870 4868, sciencemuseum.org.uk. Daily 1000-1800, closed 24-26 Dec. Free. Tube: South Kensington.

The Science Museum, which was founded in 1857, is one of the finest museums of its kind in the world and one of the best children's attractions in London. Contemplative it ain't; here kids are free to be kids, to run riot and explore to their hearts' content. The galleries, which are spread over five floors, help them do so: much of the museum is 'hands-on', attractions are well labelled and signposted (with displays low enough for even the smallest children to see), there are helpful attendants at every corner and an excellent tannoy system for connecting lost tots with worried parents. All this

Don't miss Natural History Museum

Cromwell Rd, SW7 5BD, T020-7942 5000, nhm.ac.uk. Daily 1000-1750, closed 24-26 Dec. Free except for temporary exhibitions. Tube: South Kensington.

This glorious, grand neo-Gothic meets Romanesque Victorian pile at the far end of Exhibition Road is perhaps the finest natural history museum in the world and one of London's most popular tourist draws. Its towering halls and gargantuan galleries are packed with fierce dinosaurs, fabulous interactive displays, frowsty fossils and galleries of fascinating temporary exhibitions (which have to be paid for), including the annual Veolia Environment Wildlife Photographer of the Year award. The museum can be very crowded in peak season and at weekends, and noisy with school groups at any time. It is generally at its quietest on winter and autumn weekdays. Allow a full morning for a visit.

The museum is divided into a series of colour-themed zones. The Central Hall, immediately in front of the entrance, is dominated by a huge skeleton of a diplodocus and a 1300-year-old giant sequoia. Galleries lead off from here. There are even larger whale skeletons in the **Blue Zone**, together with a life-sized model of the largest creature that has ever lived, the blue whale. The Blue Zone also houses galleries devoted to fish, amphibians, reptiles, human biology, marine invertebrates and mammals, plus the famous Dinosaur gallery, with its terrifying, roaring life-sized T-Rex, complete triceratops fossilized skeleton and hatching dino eggs. The **Green Zone** is home to stuffed birds (including a dodo and a great auk), creepy-crawlies, marine reptiles and primates, as well as displays on ecology, minerals, our place in evolution and interactive 'investigate' galleries. The creepy crawlies include all the arthropods: giant bird-eating spiders and whip scorpions (all of them dead and pinioned) and live leaf-cutter ants and cockroaches. There's a 16-ft (5-m) high walk-through termite mound, which shows how the insects keep their nests cool, and a chance to build your own arachnid. The **Red Zone** was formerly the Geological Museum (see page 66), while the **Orange Zone** is home to the Wildlife Garden and the museum's £80-million, spanking new chrysalis-like insect museum, the **Darwin Centre**, which opened in September 2009. It's an amazing structure that looks like an eight-storey termite egg bizarrely propped up against the grand Victorian building. Inside, a winding, slowly ascending walkway leads visitors past fish tank-like galleries displaying the museum's collection of over 17 million insects and arachnids, three million plant specimens and the white-coated entomologists beetling away in a working, open-plan lab. Interactive displays alongside the exhibits have the arthropods spring to life on screen, where they can be examined and scrutinized at leisure; you can magnify body parts or click on menus to find out about everything from spiracles and chitin to insect sex. There are also games and educational exhibits for kids. The ground floor of the centre houses the David Attenborough studio which hosts shows, talks and special films. Make sure you pick up a free Natural History card in the Darwin Centre; you can scan the card to collect information on the featured nature exhibits and then access them through your own museum webpage.

has led some critics to complain that the museum has dumbed down since its glory days in the 1970s. Don't believe a word of it; it has merely become more accessible to people of all ages and levels of scientific interest. Gone are the dusty displays and ageing wooden cabinets; galleries are now carefully lit and engaging, stimulating all the senses with bangs, whirrs and thuds from machinery, exhibits where you can 'smell space' and tactile displays where children don gloves to handle mock fissile material or make elaborate kaleidoscope patterns with their movements. In all, there are more than 800 state-of-the-art interactive educational displays, some of which extend over entire rooms. Kids can launch their own air rocket, take a simulated flight over a glacier, feel a dinosaur's breath or the impact of the launch of the Saturn V rocket. Opened in 2010 were the beautiful, shiny blue Atmosphere gallery and the Fly Zone, which allows visitors to experience what it's like to fly a jet, while the Legend of Apollo (£5, £4 child) attempts to give visitors a sense of what it is like to be an astronaut.

All these interactive attractions sit alongside displays of historical and technological objects from the museum's collection of more than 300,000. They include north American fire drills, Babbage's proto-computer, the first steam locomotive (Stephenson's Rocket), Formula One racing cars, aeroplanes, missiles and a replica of one of the Eagle lunar-landing modules from the Apollo missions (much of the original is still on the moon). Science and the Art of Medicine, Glimpses of Medical History and Health Matters are housed in the **Wellcome medical wing**.

Each gallery has activity areas where children and adults alike can enjoy talks and take part in demonstrations on many, constantly varying themes. It's worth asking at one of the help desks for a schedule so you can plan which activities you want to attend. The basement is the best area for younger kids; here you will find **Launchpad**, with 50 different interactive exhibits specifically for children, ranging from simple shape puzzles to more sophisticated displays. **Pattern Pod** is similar but aimed at children between five and eight years old, and **Antenna** is a gallery that profiles contemporary scientific issues of particular interest to teenagers and young people. There are

Royal Albert Hall

The Royal Albert Hall (Kensington Gore, SW7 2AP, T0845-401 5045, royalalberthall.com, tube: South Kensington), a splendid Victorian building inspired by the Coliseum in Rome, is one of the capital's most famous concert venues. It used to be joked that because of the concert hall's echo, it was the only performance space in the world where modern British composers could hear their work twice. Thankfully, a set of inverted polystyrene mushrooms hanging from the ceiling have ensured that the acoustics are now as good as the lavish neoclassical decoration, and coming to the hall for a lunchtime or evening concert is a real treat. There's always plenty to choose from, especially in the late summer when the BBC Proms (Promenade Concerts) kick off. These offer a wealth of serious and light classical performances, many of which are suitable for or aimed at children and young people. At Christmas the hall hosts a fabulous Seasonal Festival of carols and choir concerts.

free activity sessions, too, where children can make things to take home with them, like toy cars powered by elastic bands. You can even create your very own personalized website to look at when you get back home – or in the free Wi-Fi area on the ground floor, if you've brought a laptop.

Victoria & Albert Museum (V&A)

Cromwell Rd, SW7 2RL, T020-7942 2000, vam.ac.uk. Sat-Thu 1000-1745, Fri 1000-2200. Free. Tube: South Kensington.

Defining the V&A's vast collections has long been a challenge. The museum describes itself as 'the world's greatest museum of art and design', but it is neither an art gallery nor a design museum. A clue to the collection lies more in its founding principle, declared in 1863, to 'collect objects wherein Fine Art is applied to some purpose of utility'. It is an instruction that has only been very loosely adhered to since, but it roughly sums up the vast and diverse collection of 1,000,000 pieces from more than 3000 years of human history: costume, ceramics, furniture, fashion, glass, jewellery, metalwork, photography, sculpture, textiles and paintings.

Children don't bother with definitions: for them, it is a wonder emporium, a marvellous miscellany of treasures and

curios, with rooms of sparkling Elizabethan gowns or fashionable contemporary dresses and sixties' shoes; others have sparkling cases of jewellery and gems, or rows of glittering arms and armour. There's a gallery with 4000 years of twinkling glass reached by a shimmering glass staircase, rows of lavish and colourful theatrical props, and shell-like plaster casts of whole portions of European and Asian buildings brought to London in Imperial times for the delight of those who would never travel outside Britain. There's even a delightful garden patio, deep in the museum, with a tinkling fountain-filled paddling pool which children are welcome to

play in. There are 'discovery areas' too, where kids can dress up in armour or bustles and corsets, make some furniture, draw a picture or build a crystal palace. The museum gives each child visitor an activity rucksack (which must be returned on leaving the V&A). Each is different, with games, pads, magic glasses and other fun items inside. Parents need to leave ID as a deposit.

The best way to see the collection is simply to walk in and wander freely through the labyrinth of rooms. This is a museum to lose oneself in, perhaps returning another day with a clearer plan and set of objectives.

Out & about Kensington, Chelsea & Knightsbridge

Geological Museum (Earth Galleries)

Cromwell Rd, SW7 5BD, T020-7942 5000, nhm.ac.uk. Daily 1000-1750, closed 24-26 Dec. Free except for temporary exhibitions. Tube: South Kensington.

The Geological Museum is often overlooked by families in a rush to visit the adjacent Science and Natural History museums (into which it has now been nominally absorbed as the Red Zone). But it's well worth a browse. Be sure to make your way in through the eastern door (look for the sign saying 'Geological Survey Museum' carved over the entrance in Exhibition Road), ascending the escalators to pass through the centre of a brilliantly lit globe. Beyond are galleries showcasing a stunning array of some 30,000 precious and semi-precious stones (including diamonds, emeralds and some gorgeous carbuncles and tourmalines), meteors, moon rocks and interactive displays telling the story of the planet. There's a room dressed up as a Japanese convenience store where visitors can experience a simulated earthquake and a corridor linking directly to the Natural History Museum (see page 62).

Kensington Palace

Kensington Gardens, W8 4PX, T0844-482 7799, hrp.org.uk. Daily 1000-1700. £12.50, £6.25 child, £34 family. Tube: Queensway, Notting Hill Gate or High Street Kensington.

This Jacobean mansion was re-modelled by Sir Christopher Wren for William III and Mary II for their London home. Queen Victoria was born and lived here until she became queen in 1837 and the palace has long been a residence for celebrity royals and their retinue. These include Wild Peter, a completely silent boy who was found living naked in woods near Hanover in Germany. He was brought to London in the spring of 1726 and lived for a while as part of the court of George I, becoming a London celebrity. Daniel Defoe wrote a book about him and his likeness hangs on the east wall of the King's Staircase in the palace, shown standing opposite the large palace windows wearing a green coat and holding oak leafs and acorns in his right hand. After the king's death Peter's care was given to a Hertfordshire farmer. Peter lived until he was over 70 years old, healthy and happy, and, while he apparently understood what was said to him, he could only ever say the words 'Peter' and 'King George'. Princess Margaret lived here for 42 years and Diana, Princess of Wales lived at Apartment 8 Kensington Palace from the time of her wedding on 29 July 1981 until she died on 31 August 1997. The palace became famous all over the world in the days after her death: more than a million bouquets covered the front gates and the palace stayed open around the clock to cope with the 136,000 mourners that came to sign condolence books for the princess.

Much of the palace, including Queen Victoria's former bedroom, can be visited. And, true to Diana's fashion-conscious spirit, parts of the building have been transformed into 'The Enchanted Palace', a unique, phantasmagorical exhibition that looks like it has drifted out of an Angela Carter dream, and which showcases the work of some of the quirkiest names in British fashion. Exhibits include a dress of tears by Aminaka Wilmont, an installation of hats by milliner Stephen Jones, a Vivienne Westwood dress, a soundscape of ticking and chiming clocks by Boudicca, accompanied by 'dresses the colour of time' circling the room and an origami dress by William Tempest, which appears to vanish into its surroundings. The exhibition is themed around a 'quest for the seven princesses' who once lived in Kensington Palace and is aimed resolutely at girls (of all ages), who must piece together clues from the installations, to discover the identity of 'the rebellious princess who ran from an arranged marriage into the arms of love' and the 'sad queens who bore the pain and sadness of lost babies'.

National Army Museum

Royal Hospital Rd, Chelsea, SW3 4IT, T020-7730 0717, national-army-museum.ac.uk. Daily 1000-1730, closed 24-26 Dec, 1 Jan. Free. Tube: Sloane Square.

The British Army, unlike the navy and air force, is not Royal and is answerable to the British people themselves, through Parliament. This museum concentrates on personal naratives, telling the army's story from the Middle Ages to the present day, through the words and experiences of ordinary soldiers, including archers at Agincourt, battlefield privates at Waterloo and SAS troopers. It is the only military museum in the capital to cover

so long a period of history. There are poignant and touching displays which tell of the horrors of the trenches, as well as famous victories, and a heap of curious relics which bring military history to gruesome life for kids, including the saw which was used to amputate the Earl of Uxbridge's leg at Waterloo, a cat rescued from a house in Sevastopol (and later stuffed for posterity) and a modern pilotless army drone aircraft.

The museum caters very well for children, with a series of Action Zones where kids can get their hands on military equipment and play a range of quizzes, games and other activities. The Kids' Zone is one of the best museum play areas in central London and it is worth visiting for this alone. Older children can weave between forest trees, romp through assault courses or scale the walls and do battle on the ramparts of a castle-themed climbing frame. Younger visitors can play in an area crammed with soft toys. There are also dressing-up costumes, arts and crafts and children's books and board games for quieter moments.

Saatchi Gallery

Duke of York's HQ, King's Rd, SW3 4RY, T020-8968 9331, saatchi-gallery.co.uk. Daily 1000 1800. Free. Tube: Sloane Square.

Charles Saatchi, London's foremost contemporary art

collector and champion of the Young British Artists (YBAs), including Damien Hirst, opened the city's most prestigious private contemporary art gallery in late 2008. It's housed in a surprisingly understated neoclassical edifice whose capacious and minimalist interior shows some of the city's most experimental and challenging exhibitions. Kids and adults alike will either be amused or bemused by the annual repertory of shows. Some are decidedly adult in theme but the gallery actively encourages younger visitors and offers a range of activities to enhance their experience (see below). Education Packs are available online for every gallery show and provide a useful guide for young people on key works in the exhibitions.

Action stations

Activity days & workshops

The **Saatchi Gallery** (see above) takes part in the Great Art Quest, a national arts project designed by the Prince's Foundation for Children & the Arts, which aims to introduce children aged between nine and 11 to visual art, brought to life through storytelling and workshops hosted at the gallery. The gallery also runs regular drawing workshops led by experienced artists for children aged between 10 and 16,

Out & about Kensington, Chelsea & Knightsbridge

offering them the opportunity to learn observational drawing skills, experiment with a variety of media and draw from still life set-ups, as well as clothed models. All materials are provided. The programme is run in conjunction with the **Prince's Drawing School**. The **V&A** (see page 64) organizes a bewildering variety of family-orientated events, workshops and guided visits. For details, consult the website (vam.ac.uk). The **Science** (see page 61) and **Natural History museums** (see page 62) run numerous daily workshops and demonstrations, which can be booked within the museum during the course of a visit, and have a busy seasonal programme of kids' activities, which always include

sleepovers in the museums' galleries; see the websites sciencemuseum.org.uk and nhm.ac.uk for full details.

Boating

Hyde Park (royalparks.org.uk; see page 58) has rowing and pedal boats (each holding six people), which operate on the Serpentine (Easter-Oct daily 1000-sunset, £9/hr, £3/hr child) and Britain's first completely solar-powered boat, the Solarshuttle, which carries up to 40 passengers.

Riding

Hyde Park has a specialist horse-riding arena (manege) and two designated routes for horse riding. The manege is at the end of the Sports Field next to the

children's playground. Riding is available to customers and members of local stables; for details, call **Hyde Park Stables** (T020-7723 2813) or **Ross Nye Stables** (T020-7262 3791).

Swimming

In summer you can cool off at the **Serpentine Lido & Paddling Pool** (Hyde Park, T020-7706 3422, May Sat-Sun 1000-1800, Jun-12 Sep daily 1000-1800, £4, £3 concessions, £1 child, under 3s free).

Tennis

Hyde Park's **Tennis & Sports Centre** (call T020-7262 3474 for opening hours and bookings) has six tennis courts, plus a putting lawn, bowling green and café.

Pedalo power on the Serpentine.

Out & about Bloomsbury, Holborn & Covent Garden

What was once a smelly vegetable market and a breeding ground for pigs has become over the centuries London's intellectual heart: refined, literary boroughs, crammed with little boutique shops and cafés. Come here for arty shopping, cream teas and a series of wonderful museums, including Britain's biggest tourist draw, the British Museum.

Covent Garden.

Fun & free

Be entertained
The piazza, markets and narrow streets of **Covent Garden** (tube: Covent Garden or Leicester Square) are crowded with tourists at any time. They come for opera and ballet at the Royal Opera House (see page 21) and ENO (see page 21), the smart shops and cafés, the markets (see page 16) and the dozens of street performers. Kids will love the monocyclists and magicians, the jugglers and musicians (many of whom are students at London's various music schools). It's hard to believe that from medieval times to the early 20th century, this area was famous for its vast vegetable market.

Run wild
No adult can enter **Coram's Fields** (93 Guilford St, WC1N 1DN, T020-7837 6138, coramsfields.org, tube: Russell Square) without a child. When

high-brow culture gets too much, kids can rush about this seven-acre playground to their hearts' content, kick a ball on the artificial turf, splash in the paddling pools, get dirty in sandpits, whip along zip lines, stroke goats and rabbits in the pets corner or craft and create at the drop-in activity centre. The park also has a decent little vegetarian café and a nursery.

More family favourites

Cartoon Museum
35 Little Russell St, WC1A 2HH, T020-580 8155, cartoonmuseum.org. Tue-Sat 1030-1730, Sun 1200-1730, closed Mon and bank hols. £5.50, children free. Tube: Russell Square. This small gallery a stroll from the British Museum showcases the best of British cartoon and caricature since the 18th century, with images by William Hogarth, Giles, Ralph Steadman,

Gerald Scarfe and Steve Bell. There's plenty for kids who are fans of British comics, with original artwork on loan from the Beano, the Dandy and Topper, including the Bash Street Kids, Roger the Dodger, Billy the Whizz, Desperate Dan, Beryl the Peril and Dennis the Menace. The museum shop is packed with books, prints, cards and cartoon ephemera.

Dickens Museum
Doughty St, WC1N 2LX, T020-7405 2127, dickensmuseum.com. Mon-Sat 1000-1700 and over Christmas for

> 66 99
> The Cartoon Gallery is my favourite place in London. It has unusual inventions and books which I haven't seen anywhere before. I love the robots too.
>
> **Ayden, aged 10**

special Dickens-themed festive events. £6, £3 child. Tube: Russell Square.
With a home in Highgate, a drinking hole on St Katharine's Docks and plaques on every other street corner, Charles Dickens is as ubiquitous in London as London is in the author's novels and short stories. The museum, which sits in one of the author's former homes, is packed with Dickens memorabilia and hosts special exhibitions relating to his work, which are often of interest to children. In the past they have included 'Oliver from page to stage', 'Dickens' Child's History of England' and 'Katey – Dickens' artistic daughter'.

Foundling Museum
40 Brunswick Sq, WC1N 1AZ, T020-7841 3600, foundlingmuseum.org.uk. Tue-Sat 1000-1700, Sun 1100-1700, closed Mon and bank hols. £7.50, children free. Tube: Russell Square.
This small museum records and remembers the first home for abandoned children in the city, the Foundling Hospital, which was established in the early 18th century by the philanthropist Thomas Coram and governed by the cartoonist William Hogarth and the adopted Londoner and court composer, George Friedrich Handel. Heart-rending displays (which include keepsakes left by distraught, impoverished mothers, paintings and old photographs) tell the story

of the 27,000 children who passed through the hospital between 1739 and 1954. These sit alongside period interiors, artworks and the Gerald Coke Handel Collection, the largest privately held collection of Handel material in the world. The collections are housed in a restored building adjacent to the original site of the hospital, which was demolished in 1928. There are free activity backpacks for five- to eight-year-olds, each containing activities and games based on a central theme (the Sea, Animals, Meet the Foundlings or Music). There are also free trails around the museum for three- to 12-year-olds.

Freemasons' Hall
60 Great Queen St, WC2B 5AZ, T020-7831 9811. Mon-Fri 1000-1700. Free. Tube: Covent Garden or Holborn.

Young fans of Dan Brown and conspiracy theories in general should not miss what is arguably the most important and certainly the oldest Freemasons' lodge in the world: the headquarters of the United Grand Lodge of England. It's housed in a vast and imposing art deco mock temple, which somehow succeeds in being almost invisible while hulking over Covent Garden and the west side of Holborn. Guided tours show visitors around the hallowed, echoing halls, the library, central ritual and meeting hall and drawing rooms, one of which has a vast portrait of George Washington clad in full masonic garb with a glittering gold amulet around his neck.

London Transport Museum
Covent Garden Piazza, Covent Garden, WC2E 7BB, T020-7639 3744,

Out & about Bloomsbury, Holborn & Covent Garden

ltmuseum.co.uk. Mon-Thu, Sat-Sun 1000-1800, Fri 1100-1800. £13, under 16s free. Tube: Covent Garden.

This big, bright, well-presented but overpriced museum right in the heart of Covent Garden explores the history of transport in London through interactive panels, historical displays and with old vehicles (including trams and early 20th-century Routemaster buses – all of which can be clambered over by kids). The shop sells unusual and quirky souvenirs.

Pollock's Toy Museum

1 Scala St, W1T 2HL, T020-7636 3452, pollockstoymuseum.com. Mon-Sat 1000-1700, closed bank hols. £5. Tube: Goodge Street, Warren Street or Euston Square.

Pollock's is a children's museum for adults: a jumbled-up collection of toy theatres (many from Pollock's original toy theatre shop), teddy bears, dolls, board games, nursery furniture, mechanical toys and dolls' houses crammed into two tiny and rickety adjacent houses near busy Tottenham Court Road. Just over 200 years' worth of priceless and fascinating toys sit behind glass in poorly lit rooms linked by tiny corridors and creaking staircases. The shop sells quirky items, such as miniature hurdy-gurdies and forgotten children's treasures like pop and spud guns; in the shop children can handle and play with the toys.

Sir John Soane's Museum

13 Lincoln's Inn Fields, WC2A 3BP, T020-7440 4263, soane.org. Tue-Sat 1000-1700, tours Sat 1100, candlelit opening on the first Tue of each month 1800-2100, closed 24-28 Dec and 1-3 Jan. Free, tours £5. Tube: Holborn.

This eclectic phantasmagoria of paintings, artefacts and curios was assembled by one of the first great architects of the Augustan age, Sir John

Soane, an eccentric who rose from humble beginnings (as a mason's son) to a Royal Academy medal and architectural commissions by the time he was 19. He was the foremost neoclassical architect of the late 18th century, responsible for the (sadly butchered) Bank of England, Pitzhanger Place in Ealing and the Dulwich Picture Gallery, among others. The museum, which was his own home, was one of his greatest creations. It has an ingenious, Chinese box of an interior, with folding walls (allowing for a choice of priceless Canalettos to be displayed), double-height spaces and arches rising to glass roof-lights whose reflections are caught by an elaborate network of mirrors and which lend the house an ethereal glow. Each room seems to be a chamber from Soane's fantastical imagination. Hogarth's famous *Rake's Progress* hangs in the Picture Room, alongside Turner oil paintings and depictions of scenes from Shakespeare. Other walls are covered in classical busts, astronomical clocks and Chinese tiles, and a sepulchral basement houses the sarcophagus of the Egyptian Pharaoh Seti I, a mummy's head and the desiccated carcasses of dozens of cats pulled from the walls of London houses by Soane's workers. (The cats were entombed in the walls by medieval Londoners

who believed a cat corpse permanently warded off rodents.) The room's Gothic horror atmosphere is played upon by the staff conducting the wonderful candlelit tour, who allow children to put their hands in a bag of squidgy eyeballs, which are, in reality, lychees.

Action stations

Activity days & workshops
The **British Museum** (see page 72) organizes regular family days and a whole host of events for kids. These include the exciting Night in the Museum sleepovers when children can spend the night with the creepy mummies and museum ghosts; check the website for full details (britishmuseum.org). The **Cartoon Museum** (see page 74) has a young artists' gallery, where children can draw their own cartoons. It also runs an annual Young Cartoonists of the Year competition and organizes animation classes and family fun days, which can be booked through the website (cartoonmuseum.org). The **Foundling Museum** (see page 71) has family days, with craft activities for children aged three to 12 years old, usually on the first Saturday of each month and on Thursdays and Fridays during school holidays, when children and up to two accompanying adults gain free entry to the museum; see the website for full details (foundlingmuseum.org.uk). The museum also has drop-in sessions with a similar range of activities; arrive early to ensure a place. **Coram's Fields** (see page 70) offer a seasonal programme of activities and workshops all of which are advertised on their website (coramsfields.org).

Don't miss British Museum

Great Russell St, WC1B 3DG, T020-7323 8181, britishmuseum.org. Daily 1000-1730. Free except for special shows. Tube: Tottenham Court Road or Russell Square.

The British Museum is quite simply one of the finest museums anywhere. Its collections of antiquities, gleaned from the entire globe and dating back to the dawn of human history, are unrivalled and include the sculptures from the Parthenon, the Rosetta Stone, Lohan Buddhas from China, Easter Island stone heads, stele from Mayan temples and a trove of treasures from Mesopotamia, Persia, ancient Europe and Asia. Since Neil MacGregor took over the directorship in 2002, the big annual exhibitions have been as bold and spectacular as those at the New York Met, with the cream of the museum's collection sitting alongside treasures from other world-class collections in themed exhibitions that have proved immensely popular with visitors of all ages. They have helped the British Museum to become Britain's biggest tourist attraction, with more than six million visitors a year.

Like many of London's museums and galleries, the British Museum began principally as a private collection given to the nation in 1753 by the Ulster physician and inventor of chocolate milkshakes, Hans Sloane, after whom Sloane Square is named. Money to purchase Montagu House (a townhouse which stood on the current site) was raised by national lottery in 1754. George II added the entire Royal Library to the collection in 1757 and, in 1801, the British Army added Egyptian artefacts captured from Napoleon in Alexandria. Elgin added the bas reliefs plucked from the Parthenon in 1815 and, by the 1840s, the collection had grown so large it required a new building, constructed by the adventurer and neoclassicist Robert Smirke. The Museum has never been exclusive or highbrow and has been loved by children since Victorian times, when they apparently wandered in off the foggy streets and explored unfettered. Elizabeth Cook comments in *Highways and Byways in London*, written at the turn of the 19th century, that "rows of chattering little girls in pinafores, corresponding little boys in knickerbockers, greet one at every turn." She remembers a conversation between a group of girls in the Greek galleries: "'Ere's the Wenus', one will say: 'you can always tell 'er, 'cos she seems to be lookin' round and sayin', 'Ain't I pretty?'". And, over a mummy's tomb, some poor London boys: "'Ere, look 'ere Jimmy.... You can see the corpse's 'ole fice! Blimy if 'e ain't 'ad 'is nose bruk in a fight, as 'e ain't got but the 'alf of it left.'" Little has changed today, though the languages are now legion.

Cook also remarked that "People who find the British

Museum exhausting – and there are many – take too much of it at one time." There is simply too much to see in one visit, and far too much to describe here even in adequate outline. The best strategy is to begin with a perusal of the excellent museum website and, in particular, the 'young explorer' and 'plan your visit' pages, and then pick up a free floorplan from reception on arrival. Themed family trail plans (taking from 30 mins to 1 hr) and activity backpacks (deposit £10) are available from the Paul Hamlyn library next to the gift shop.

A new World Conservation & Exhibitions Centre designed by Richard Rogers will open in early 2012. This will be a dedicated gallery for the museum's lavish special exhibitions. Note that the Ford Centre near reception has baby feeding and nappy-changing facilities as well as a play space.

Ground floor highlights

★ The Great Court, with its spectacular glass roof designed by Norman Foster.

★ The famous circular Reading Room, where Marx wrote much of *Das Kapital*.

★ Egyptian royal tombs, mummies and the Rosetta Stone.

★ Greek and Roman sculpture, including the infamous Elgin marbles from the Parthenon.

★ Royal Lion Hunt bas reliefs from Nineveh in Assyria.

★ Temple sculptures from India.

★ Thai and Chinese Buddhist sculptures, including the mesmerizing Lohan Buddhas.

★ Chinese ceramics.

★ Lintels from Yaxchilán in Mayan Mexico and an Aztec stone knife probably used in human sacrifices.

Upper floor highlights

★ Japanese ceramics, carvings and Samurai armour.

★ The Egyptian tomb-chapel of Nebamun.

★ Exhibits from Roman and pre-Roman Britain, including the stunning Hinton St Mary floor mosaic and Lindow man, nicknamed Pete Marsh after being pulled from one some 2300 years after his death.

★ Exhibits from medieval Europe, including the Lewis chessmen, shields and swords.

★ Exhibits from ancient Iran, Turkey and Mesopotamia, including cuneiform tablets and a circa 2700-year-old map of the world.

★ Exhibits from the Roman Empire, including the famous cameo glass Portland Vase.

Lower floor highlights

★ Exhibits from Africa, with magnificent pieces from the Ife kingdom of Nigeria.

★ Exhibits from ancient Greece and Rome, with fragments from Erechtheum and the Nike temple from the Parthenon.

It makes me feel excited looking at objects centuries old and the British Museum has one extremely famous artefact, the Rosetta Stone. It also has a great shop with amazing books.

Lucas, aged 10

Out & about City of London

The square mile of the City is where London makes its money. Most of the world's great banks have a major headquarters here and the area's wealth is evident in streets of grand Imperial buildings, including St Paul's and the Bank of England, and clusters of sparkling skyscrapers like the famous Gherkin, the Lloyd's building and, just across the river, the new Shard – the tallest building in the European Union. The best way for kids to enjoy the views are from the medieval ramparts of the Tower of London, the dome of St Paul's or from a Thames river boat.

Hit or miss?

Bank of England Museum
Threadneedle St, EC2R 8AH, T020-7601 5545, bankofengland. co.uk. Mon-Fri 1000-1700 (last entry 1645), Christmas Eve 1000-1300, closed Sat-Sun and bank hols. Free. Tube: Bank.

Children will be most impressed by the real Roman and modern-day gold bars (which they can attempt to lift) in this tiny museum devoted to the history of banking in London. Grown-ups will also appreciate the beautiful vaulted roof with its glass skylights by Sir John Soane.

Dr Johnson's House
17 Gough Sq, EC4A 3DE, T020-7353 3745, drjohnsonshouse. org. Oct-Apr Mon-Sat 1100-1700, May-Sep Mon-Sat 1100-1730. £4.50, £1.50 child. Tube: Chancery Lane.

The London home of the famous man of letters sits in a peaceful square between the city and Chancery Lane. It's where he compiled his famous dictionary and is one of the best preserved 18th-century townhouses in London, though both facts may be of dubious interest to children, who will be more interested in trying on the period costumes.

Big days out

St Paul's Cathedral
St Paul's Churchyard, EC4M 8AD, T020-7246 8350, stpauls.co.uk. Mon-Sat 0830-1600. £12.50, £4.50 child, including multimedia guides and a guided tour. Tube: St Paul's.
If Westminster Abbey is the soul of Westminster and the chapel of kings and statesmen, then St Paul's is the heart of the City of London and an expression in stone of the pomp and prosperity of the Empire. A cathedral on this site has been a statement of the power of Britain and one of the most enduring symbols of London since Saxon times. It is a magnificent, opulent building, topped by a splendid dome 100 ft (30 m) above the nave. Children love climbing up the vertiginous steps to the famous whispering gallery, whose acoustics are so perfect that it is possible to have a clear conversation from one side of the cupola to the other. You can continue up from here to the exterior Golden Gallery at the very top of the dome, from where there are stunning panoramas across London. The building's history and litter of monuments might pass all but the older children by, but none can fail to be impressed by the confident grandeur of the interior, the dizzying height of the dome and the wonderful views out over the city.

St Paul's has long been a sacred site. There was probably a temple to Diana here or very close by in Roman times – effigies to the goddess have been unearthed near the cathedral – and it is possible that there was a small Christian temple here, erected by two missionaries from Rome in the second century. The current building by Sir Christopher Wren is the third cathedral to stand on the site. The first two were Catholic: a Saxon edifice, built around 604 AD, and a Norman one with Gothic flourishes that was by far the biggest building in Britain, far larger than Wren's cathedral. London spread at its feet and spilt through its many colleges and halls into the church itself, with Londoners playing ball games, staging wrestling matches and even selling beer at stalls and trotting horses down the nave. Wren had been commissioned to renovate the old cathedral in 1663, which

St Paul's and the Millennium Bridge.

was crumbling and which had lost its spire in a thunderstorm. He hated the building and must have been relieved when it burnt down in the Great Fire of 1666, leaving 200 ft (60 m) of the tower. Wren pressed for complete demolition and, together with his master builder, Edward Strong, and clerk of works, Nicholas Hawksmoor, set about building a new building on Italian neoclassical lines – a plan which was condemned as being too 'popish' by many in London's establishment. The first stone was laid in 1675 and the cathedral finished in 1710, when Wren was 78 years old. The church's importance as a national symbol is reflected in its cost: £750,000, more than a billion pounds in today's money. It was paid for by tax levied on sea-borne coal.

St Paul's crypt and chapels are crammed with monuments to the great men and women of British history. A cluster of fragmented tombs in the crypt hold the remains recovered from the previous St Paul's, such as Francis Bacon's father, Sir Nicholas Bacon. Admiral Lord Nelson and the Duke of Wellington lie in magnificent tombs of state in the crypt, alongside TE Lawrence (of Arabia) and Christopher Wren himself. A host of British Imperial heroes include Nelson's Trafalgar compatriot Vice Admiral Lord Collingwood,

Out & about City of London

Lieutenant-General Sir Ralph Abercromby (who defeated Napoleon in Alexandria), Major General Charles Gordon (who sacked Beijing and burned the Imperial Summer Palace and Gardens of Perfect Brightness) and Field Marshall Lord Kitchener, Secretary of State for War during World War I. Look out for Sir Joshua Reynolds pontificating to the Royal Academy and John Howard, the Augustan philanthropist responsible for creating modern prisons, who is depicted trampling on marble fetters at the entrance to the choir, next to a statue of a half-naked, unhappy-looking Dr Johnson. The apse of the cathedral is home to the American Memorial Chapel, built in 1958, to honour American soldiers who died in World War II.

Where's the fire?

66 99

The Bank of England is a fun place for all ages. They understand that kids will be there so they add things that won't be boring. You can feel a gold bar and control hot air balloons. It makes me feel really good.

Edward, aged nine

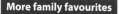
More family favourites

Museum of London
London Wall, EC2Y 5HN, T020-7001 9844, museumoflondon.org.uk. Mon-Sat 1000-1800, closed 24-26 Dec 24-26. Free. Tube: Barbican, St Paul's or Moorgate.
If you are new to London and want to get acquainted with the city, then make this museum your first port of call. A series of imaginative, modern galleries with state-of-the-art interactive exhibits tell the story of London from the Stone Age to modern times. The museum does its

utmost to be kid-friendly and bring history alive. Kids can wander through a Roman living room, a wattle-and-daub house, a Victorian shop, a dank cell from Newgate prison or a World War II Anderson bomb shelter, with associated sound effects along the way. Scale models show the first St Paul's Cathedral (which perished in the Great Fire), interactive digital maps bring London to life, allowing kids to explore different areas and zoom in on

particular attractions, panels add more written and photographic detail, while others show films or project images, and cases display artefacts including beautiful pieces unearthed at the Roman temple to Mithras in the City of London. There's also an 18th-century pleasure garden and an interactive map of the Thames showing how London's skyline is changing with high-rise buildings and modernist architecture. The museum underwent extensive refurbishment in the first decade of the millennium, opening five new 'Galleries of Modern London' in May 2010, costing a total of £18 million. These sit in a stunning glass cube perched over the street and tell the story of the city from the Great Fire of London in 1666 to the present day. There's a lavish gilt Lord Mayor's coach, gritty displays showcasing the troubled 1970s and 1980s (with the rise of the fascist National Front and the poll tax riots) and cutesier items like an old two-penny red phone box, which was once as much a London icon as the black cab.

Visits can be self-guided, or it's possible to take a guided tour with cockney 'Pearly King', John Walters, who gives a colourful running commentary dressed from head to toe in traditional East End pearly buttons and a black cap.

Action stations

Activities & workshops

The **Barbican Centre** (Silk St, EC2Y 8DS, T020-7638 8891, barbican.org.uk, tube: Barbican) is one of Europe's largest multi-arts venues and boasts one of the capital's most eclectic and diverse menus of daytime and evening concerts, arts events, festivals, film and fashion shows, many of which are suitable for, or specifically geared towards, families; see the website for full details.

The Gherkin.

EC3N 4AB, hrp.org.uk/towerof london. Mar-Oct Tue-Sat 0900-1730, Sun-Mon 1000-1730 (last entry 1700), Nov-Feb Tue-Sat 0900-1630, Sun-Mon 1000-1630 (last entry 1600), closed 24-26 Dec and 1 Jan. £18.70, £15.9 concessions, £10.45 under 16s, under 5s free, £51.70 family (prices include a voluntary donation; discounts for online bookings up to 7 days in advance). Tube: Tower Hill.

As a historic landmark and symbol of London the Tower takes its place alongside the Houses of Parliament and St Paul's Cathedral. And, like both, it is a statement in stone of the indomitable power of the state. William the Conqueror's first stone structure, the 100-ft (30-m) tall White Tower was completed 24 years after the Battle of Hastings, its bulk imposed on early medieval London and its 16-ft (5-m) thick walls standing over deep dungeons. It was

Murders in the dark:
the bloody history of the Tower

As the power of the Normans grew and became more firmly entrenched, the White Tower went from fortress to bloody gaol. It was expanded into a castle under William of Longchamp in the 1100s. Henry III added further fortifications and the infamous Traitors' Gate in the 1260s and, by the 1300s, the Tower had grown huge and seemingly impregnable: a refuge for royals and their retinue. Then, it was breached during Wat Tyler's peasant's revolt in 1381, when the Archbishop of Canterbury was dragged from St John's Chapel in the White Tower to meet his death on Tower Hill. This led subsequent monarchs to fortify the Tower still further. Not that it served them well. Henry VI spent much of the War of the Roses in the castle, but died in mysterious circumstances in the Wakefield Tower. Richard of Gloucester, later Richard III, allegedly murdered his rivals to the throne, the 12-year-old Prince Edward and his 10-year-old brother, in the infamous Bloody Tower. His successors, the Tudors, continued the blood-letting. Henry VIII had two of his wives beheaded here, along with Sir Thomas More and a number of dissenting bishops. Mary executed Lady Jane Grey (who came to pray in the Chapel of St John the night before she died) and Guildford Dudley, and Elizabeth executed Sir Walter Raleigh, after his various ill-fated trips to Venezuela in search of *El Dorado* all but bankrupted the Treasury. King James I had Guy Fawkes, the gunpowder plotter, imprisoned and tortured here in 1605, before he was hung, drawn and quartered in Westminster. After this, the Tower slipped from Royal control and ceased to be a gaol. The last execution in the Tower of London took place at 0712 on 31 January, 1941, when German parachutist Josef Jakobs was shot by firing squad. The last prisoner to be detained here was his commanding officer, Rudolf Hess, for four days in 1941.

greatly expanded by subsequent monarchs who used it as a royal residence. The fortress has played a central role in the English collective imagination, invariably associated with treachery, torture and public execution (see 'Murders in the dark' box, above).

Visiting the Tower can still be torture, especially on a hot day in high season when the crowds get so overwhelming that it can be difficult to see anything. The best way to negotiate the narrow stairs and crowds is to join one of the free Beefeater tours (every 30 mins till 1530

in summer or 1430 in winter), conducted by the colourfully dressed red-and-black yeomen warders who have been guarding the Tower, prisoners and, most significantly, the **Crown Jewels** since 1485. These tours visit all the highlights, including the jewels, the chapels

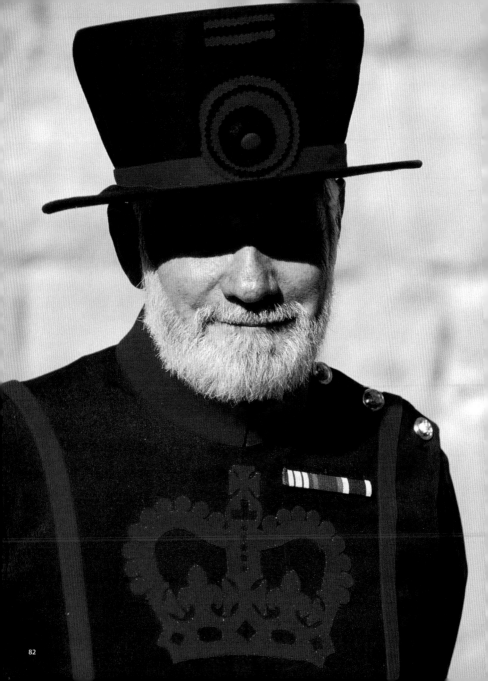

and towers, and the Beefeaters always have fascinating stories to tell. If touring independently, try to arrive at the Tower as early as possible and go straight to the Crown Jewels in the Wakefield Tower (where Henry VI is said to have been stabbed by Richard Crookback while he knelt at prayers). Most of the collection dates from after the Civil War of 1642. Alongside orbs, rings and other items of ceremonial state are two principal crowns – the 2.2-kg St Edward's Crown, which is used for the Coronation ceremony, and the Imperial State Crown, topped by the magnificent St Edward's Sapphire (said to have been taken from the ring of St Edward the Confessor) and the Cullinan II, the fourth largest polished diamond in the world, which was cut from the 3106.75 carat Cullinan, the largest rough diamond ever discovered. The larger portion of this stone forms the second largest polished diamond in the world, the Cullinan I, which sits on top of the Sceptre with the Cross. (The largest cut diamond in the world, the Golden Jubilee Diamond, forms part of the Crown Jewels of the Thai King Bhumibol Adulyadej.)

Outside the Wakefield Tower, look for the Tower's famous jet-black ravens. Legend says that the kingdom and the Tower will fall if the six resident birds ever leave the fortress. To ensure that this doesn't happen all of them have their wings clipped. At one point there were nine ravens: Raven George was fired from his post for eating television aerials and Raven Grog left the premises and was last seen outside an East End pub. The remaining seven are big powerful birds and should not be fed or approached too closely by children.

Next, move on to the **White Tower**, where children will enjoy the large collection of arms and armour (and torture paraphernalia). In the record room there are fragments of the first Zeppelin bombs dropped on London during World War II. The White Tower's chapel of St John is the simplest, earliest and most complete Norman church in Britain. William the Conqueror himself prayed here and 'Bloody' Mary was married here by proxy to Philip of Spain. Sir Walter Raleigh was imprisoned for many years in the tiny cell at the eastern end of the chapel crypt. The nave is said to be haunted by the teenage ghost of Lady Jane Grey, who was beheaded outside on Tower Green.

Climb the winding stairs of the **Beauchamp Tower**, built by Edward III (but named after Thomas Beauchamp, Earl of Warwick, who was imprisoned here in 1397) to see walls covered in graffiti carved by medieval prisoners. An elaborate inscription to the right of the fireplace was cut by teenager John Dudley, the eldest son of the Duke of Northumberland, who was imprisoned and executed here together with his father and four brothers for conspiring in favour of Lady Jane Grey. A passageway known as 'Elizabeth's Walk' connects this tower with the **Bell Tower**, where Queen Elizabeth I was imprisoned by her sister.

The small room at the foot of the stairs in the **Bloody Tower** is said to be where the two boy princes allegedly murdered by Richard III are buried. Other prisoners of the Tower include Thomas Cranmer and Judge Jeffreys, who drank himself to death here.

In addition to Beefeater tours, the Tower offers audio guides, themed family trails and fun days (with all activities included in the entrance price). It is also possible to attend the **Ceremony of the Keys**, the traditional locking-up of the Tower, which has taken place every night at 2130 for at least 700 years. Tickets are issued free of charge but requests to attend must be made in writing at least two months in advance; send a self-addressed envelope together with the requisite British postage stamps or a minimum of two international reply coupons to: Ceremony of the Keys Office, Tower of London, London, EC3N 4AB.

Contents

North London

Alexandra Palace.

You must

❶ Fly a kite on Hampstead Heath.

❷ Pose with famous faces in Madame Tussaud's.

❸ Investigate Sherlock Holmes' Baker Street home.

❹ Pet llamas in Golders Hill Park.

❺ Go wild in the country in Epping Forest.

❻ Fly a plane at the RAF Museum.

❼ Wander and watch wildlife on Regent's Canal.

❽ Shop till you drop in Camden Market.

❾ Be a bookworm in the British Library.

❿ Marvel at a Hindu mandir in Wembley.

In a report for Henry I in the late 12th century, William FitzStephen, a clerk to Thomas à Becket, described North London as "made up of tilled fields, pastures, and pleasant, level meadows with streams flowing through them, where watermill wheels turned by the current make a pleasing sound. Not far off spreads out a vast forest, its copses dense with foliage concealing wild animals – stags, does, boars, and wild bulls."

Although much of FitzStephen's description has disappeared under houses, north London is still the most heavily wooded of London's regions. And, whereas in much of the south, parks seem to squeeze in between dense swathes of streets, in the north, streets and boroughs squeeze in between the parks. Remnants of the great Middlesex forest remain in Highgate and contiguous **Queen's Wood**, where there are more squirrels and hedgehogs than visiting people. Even close to central London, ranks of stately Regency townhouses are defined by a string of green spaces: lovely **Regent's Park** with its rose gardens, lakes and famous zoo; **Primrose Hill** with its magnificent, sweeping views of the city, and **Hampstead Heath**, London's most glorious green space, large enough to get lost on and wonderful for sledging or flying a kite. Urban north London clusters around the edges of these parks; the hippie markets and museums of **Camden** are bisected by a glorious artery of green, the **Regent's Canal**, busy with barge boats, ducks and herons; the literary streets of **Hampstead** and **Highgate** feel like country villages broken by Hampstead Heath, and even the buses and fumes of bustling Baker Street, home to **Madame Tussaud's** and the **Sherlock Holmes Museum**, fade in a few minutes into birdsong on adjacent Regent's Park.

Hide and seek on Hampstead Heath.

Fun & free

Picnic in the park

Regent's Park (royalparks.gov.
uk, Jan 0500-1700, Feb 0500-
1800, Mar 0500-1900, Apr and
Aug 0500-2100, May-Jul 0500-
2130, Sep 0500-2000, Oct 0500-
1730, Nov-Dec 0500-1630, free,
tube: Regent's Park) is one of
the largest and most attractive
green spaces within easy reach
of Central London. Expanses of
lawn, interspersed with formal
gardens, boating ponds and
little groves of woodland, all
lend it a far more intimate feel
than Hyde Park or Kensington
Gardens. Although it had been a
hunting ground since medieval
times, when it was part of
the great forest of Middlesex,
the park in its present form is
a creation of John Nash, the
Regency architect responsible
for revitalizing central London
in the early 19th century. He

Regent's Park.

also built the long terraces of
magnificent stucco-fronted villas
which surround the park. The
park itself shelters a number of
lavish mansions, including six
delightful fantasy villas in the
northwestern corner, designed
by Prince Charles' favourite
architects, Quinlan Terry. The
grandest home of all is **Winfield
House**, a 1930s mock-Georgian
manor set in 12 acres of private
gardens: the largest in central
London after Buckingham
Palace. It was commissioned
and lived in by Barbara Hutton
– 'the woman who blew the
Woolworths billions' – until
1946, when she sold it to the
US government for a dollar.
The mansion is now the official
residence of the United States
Ambassador and visiting US
Presidents regularly stay there.

Regent's Park is particularly
delightful in spring, when
the beds and by-ways are

coloured by a florescence of
tulips, hyacinths, daffodils and
other spring bulbs, and when
crocuses and snowdrops are
scattered across the grassy
slopes. It's the perfect place
for a picnic; pick up supplies
from the **Ferreira Delicatessen**
(see page 185), 100 m from the
park, which sells sandwiches,
cheeses, salads, fruit, figs and
freshly baked bread as well as
delicious Portuguese custard
tarts. The park is dotted with
children's playgrounds and there
are activities for children and
young adults all year round,
but especially in summer, when
the Regent's Park Open Air
Theatre sets up stage, and the
Hub sports ground reverberates
with the thwack of cricket and
softball bats. At the far northern
end of the park are London Zoo
(see page 94) and the Regent's
Canal (see page 89), both
attractions in their own right.

Spot celebrities

Immediately to the north of Regent's Park across Albert Road is **Primrose Hill**, an equally delightful but far smaller and wilder park. Climb through the little coppices to the grassy hill at its centre for one of the finest views in London: out over the chimneys and tiles, across Regent's Park, over the West End to the glistening towers of the City of London. The hill is a favourite spot for winter-time sledging and for celebrity-spotting; the infamous Primrose Hill posse of supermodels, actresses and their cohorts (the likes of Kate Moss, Sienna Miller and Sadie Frost) live nearby and can occasionally be seen recuperating from the night before in the nouveau-chic rustic cafés which litter the nearby streets.

Be a bookworm

The **British Library** (96 Euston Rd, NW1 2DB, T0843-208 1144, bl.uk, Mon and Wed-Fri 0930-1800, Tue 0930-2000, Sat 0930-1730, Sun 1100-1700, free, tube: King's Cross St Pancras) preserves the world's largest collection of printed and recorded material in a vast red-brick building next to St Pancras station. Some 150 million items are held here, including 14 million books, 920,000 journal and newspaper titles, 58 million patents and three million sound recordings. Amongst these are some of the world's literary treasures, including the Magna Carta, a Gutenberg Bible, the Lindisfarne Gospels, Leonardo da Vinci's Notebooks and Shakespeare's First Folio. Many are on permanent display in the **Sir John Ritblat Gallery**. The library also hosts at least three concurrent temporary exhibitions and storytelling workshops.

Stroll along the canal

The **Regent's Canal** is one of John Nash's lesser-known Regency creations, built to ferry goods and provisions from Paddington railway station to the Thames at Limehouse. Nowadays prettily painted barges lie moored along its banks, and herons and ducks wade in its waters. The canal bisects London, offering a historical cross-section of the city as it passes old Victorian warehouses, quaint pubs, elegant mansions, walls of graffiti by the likes of Banksy, bustling markets and modernist edifices housing TV studios or swanky designer flats. It rises and falls through Georgian locks and is lined for its entire length with a tow path, which is tranquil during the week (though watch for whizzing bicycles) and which promises an interesting walk that can be explored in its own right or as alternative route between Camden Town and London Zoo or Primrose Hill. (For details of guided walks, see page 101.) It is even possible to grab a Boris bike (www.tfl.gov.uk; see also page 172) and head all the way east to Canary Wharf (through Islington, Shoreditch, Hackney and Stepney) or west through Wembley to Windsor Castle and beyond. The route can be followed on an A-Z map or Ordnance Survey Landranger 176.

Regent's Canal.

See art in the park

Although pocket-sized
Waterlow Park (waterlowpark.
org.uk, tube: Archway or
Highgate) in Highgate village
is a delightful little oasis of
green next to the busy Archway
Road, it is only worth making
a special trip here to see the
**London International Gallery
of Children's Art** (Waterlow Park
Centre, Dartmouth Park Hill, N19
5JF, T020-7281 1111, ligca.org,
Fri-Sun 1000-1600, free). This is
the only exhibition space in the
city dedicated solely to showing
children's art. There are pieces
from every corner of the world
on show in a series of special
exhibitions and the gallery runs
event-themed workshops for
children at weekends. Also in
the park is **Lauderdale House**
(Waterlow Park, Highgate
Hill, N6 5HG, T020-0348 8716,
lauderdalehouse.org.uk, Mon-Fri
1000-1700, free), a delightful
16th-century country house,
originally built as a private home
for three-times Lord Mayor of
London, Sir Richard Martin,
which hosts a range of art
exhibitions, musical events
and weekend workshops.

Visit a country estate

Combine great art and the
great outdoors with a visit to
Kenwood House (Hampstead
Lane, NW3 7JR, englishheritage.
org.uk, daily 1130-1600, closed
24-26 Dec and 1 Jan, free).
This stately Palladian mansion

Shri Sanatan Hindu Mandir.

house designed by Robert
Adam is set in beautiful wooded
gardens on the northeastern
edge of Hampstead Heath
and is packed with priceless
art. There are fine paintings by
Rembrandt, Vermeer, Turner and
Gainsborough, and the Suffolk
collection of rare Elizabethan
portraits. It is also famous for
its elegant Adam library. All of

> **66 99**
> Kenwood has lovely views and
> there is delicious food in the
> café (all the food is fairtrade). In
> addition it is wonderful to be
> out in the fresh air and it doesn't
> matter if it is summer or winter
> because it is fun all year round.
> Being at Kenwood makes me feel
> happy, alive and I enjoy it very
> much. I highly recommend it to
> all the family.
>
> **Kaya, aged 11**

this can be perused after the
children have had a romp in the
beautiful landscaped parkland
of Hampstead Heath, with its
rhododendron groves, towering
old oaks and beeches, and some
fantastic views of the distant,
shimmering city.

Marvel at a Hindu temple

North London has two of the
most lavish and enchanting
Hindu temples outside Asia.
The stunning **Shri Sanatan
Hindu Mandir** (Ealing Rd, HA0
4TA, T020-8903 7737, svnuk.
org, daily 0800-1800, free, tube:
Alperton) in Wembley is covered
in elaborate carving, crafted in the
Indian state of Gujarat, shipped
to London and reassembled. It
looks like something from an
Indian fairy tale and is every bit as
impressive as the temples in the
sub-continent. About half a mile

Down on the farm

It might come as a surprise to many that London is dotted with small community farms. There are more than a dozen in the capital, most of which are purely recreational and aimed at letting kids get up close to livestock and small furry creatures, but a few of which produce their own organic foods. Farm Garden (farmgarden. org.uk) has a full listing but these are a few of our favourites.

Kentish Town City Farm (1 Cressfield Close, off Grafton Rd, NW5 4BN, T020-7916 5421, ktcityfarm.org.uk, daily 0900-1700, free, donations welcome) was London's first city farm and it remains one of the few that doesn't feel like a zoo for farm animals. Children are given a feel for agricultural life and encouraged to get involved in genuine farmyard activities like feeding the chickens and mucking out the stables. There's plenty of touchy, furry stuff too and many free or exceptionally good-value activities, including riding (see page 100).

Belmont Children's Farm (The Ridgeway, next to Sheepwash Pond, Mill Hill NW7 1QT, T020-8959 3308, belmontfarm.co.uk, Mon-Fri 0800-1800, Sat-Sun 0900-1800, £4.50, £2 child, under 3s free, tube: Mill Hill East and then 10 mins in a taxi) is a mini-zoo with alpacas, wallabies, reindeer and snowy owls alongside farmyard animals and cuddly pets.

Freightliners Farm (Sheringham Rd, N7 8PF, T020-7609 0467, freightlinersfarm.org.uk, Tue-Sun free) is a working farm in the urban heart of Islington, surrounded by pretty ornamental gardens, with rare breeds of cows, sheep, pigs, goats and poultry. Children can play with rabbits and learn about bees at the apiaries, and parents can buy fresh farm produce from the shop.

Hackney City Farm (1a Goldsmith's Row, E2 8QA, T020-7729 6381, hackneycityfarm.co.uk, Tue-Sun 1000-1630, free, tube: Bethnal Green, then 15-min walk) is one of London's longest established city farms, getting children, adults and farm animals together for 20 years and organizing environmental and craft-based activities, including pottery, food growing, upholstery and bee-keeping. The farm has a good restaurant and deli too.

Mudchute Farm (Pier St, Isle of Dogs, E14 3HP, T020-7515 5901, mudchute.org, Tue-Sun 0900-1700, free, DLR Mudchute, Crossharbour & Island Gardens) sits in the shadow of Canada Tower, it is the largest city farm in London, with 32 acres of rolling fields and woodland, and over 200 farm animals as well as poultry, llamas, an aviary and a pets' corner. The farm has a playground, a riding school, and a great little wholefood café, the Mudchute Kitchen.

Don't miss Hampstead Heath

Hampstead Heath (hampsteadheath.net, daily 24 hrs, free) is the wildest and most exciting of London's large parks, with countless little woods, secret gardens and hidden groves to explore, a sweeping view at every turn and some of the best children's sports and leisure facilities in the capital. The park is a large chunk of some 791 acres of ancient rough grass and moorland, interspersed with equally ancient patches of woodland and pocked with dozens of ponds, some of which were created by the damming of the River Fleet (whose course now runs underground, discharging into the Thames by Blackfriars Bridge). The Heath is large enough to get lost in and, although there are maps dotted around the periphery, it is as well to bring your own, easily downloadable from the website. Plan to spend at least half a day here, with lunch or supper in nearby **Hampstead**, a pretty village within London, famous for its literary set (see box, opposite).

The Heath divides into discrete sections. The most popular area is the southeastern corner around the famous lookout point at **Parliament Hill** (tube: Belsize Park, rail Hampstead Heath or Gospel Oak). Views from here of the towers and shards of the City are the best in North London. The hill is a favourite spot to fly a kite or sit for a picnic. A little to the east are the famous **Hampstead Ponds**, where intrepid Londoners swim with moorhens and coot (see page 101). Parliament Hill also boasts a children's adventure playground, near which there is a summer funfair.

The northern portion of the Heath is wilder and more heavily wooded, stretching up to **Hampstead Lane**, an old medieval road running between Hampstead and Highgate villages. Dick Turpin, the famous highwayman, is said to have robbed carriages along this route, a story perpetuated (along with others relating to Keats, Shelly and Dickens) by the 16th-century **Spaniards Inn** (thespaniardshampstead.co.uk), which has heavy oak panelling, hearty food, a splendid beer garden and is one of the few pubs in London to welcome children. North of Hampstead Lane, wooded lanes, which could be in the Weald of rural Kent, take you past cottages that were once home to the likes of William Blake (and still house many a famous name) to **Hampstead Garden Suburbs**. These leafy streets nestle around the lawns of the **Hampstead Heath Extension**, less visited and equally as pretty as the Heath proper, which resound to the thwack of leather balls on cricket bats in summer. Look out for the imposing

> **❝❞**
> My favourite thing is to climb trees on Hampstead Heath. I like it because it gives me a bit of time to myself whilst I'm doing something I really enjoy. It makes me feel very calm.
> **Jacob, aged 11**

mock-Rhineland Gothic church of **St Jude-on-the-Hill** (stjudeonthehill.com). Grown-ups will recognize it as a listed Edwin Lutyens building, children as the church outside Hermione Granger's parents' house in the film of *Harry Potter and the Deathly Hallows*. The church is used as a location for some BBC Prom concerts.

Tucked away at the northwestern corner of Hampstead Heath is **Golders Hill Park** (West Heath Av, NW11, T020-8455 5183, tube: Hampstead or Golders Green), a pretty, well-manicured park that is very popular with local families, who are drawn by the great little café (serving a range of hand-made ice creams), the large lawns, playground (with climbing frames, swings and tree trunks to clamber over) and the children's zoo. This last is home to grazing roe deer, alpacas and Patagonian mara, which look like giant short-eared rabbits on stilts. There are also tennis courts, golf practice nets and a bandstand, which hosts free weekend concerts

Poets' corner

There must be something in the Hampstead air that inspires poetry. Many of the country's finest wordsmiths are former residents, including Samuel Taylor Coleridge, Lord Byron, TS Eliot and John Betjeman. Shelley is said to have scribbled verse in the Spaniards Inn (see opposite) and a blue plaque marks William Blake's former home between the Heath and Heath Extension. Only one poet's former home is open to visitors, however. **Keats House** (Keats Grove, NW3 2RR, T020-7332 3868, keatshouse. cityoflondon.gov.uk, Nov-Apr Fri-Sun 1300-1700, May-Oct Tue-Sun 1300-1700, £5, £3 concessions, under 16s free, tube: Hampstead or Belsize Park), a handsome Georgian townhouse in Hampstead village, is where the famous Romantic lived between 1818 and 1820 and wrote many of his most distinguished poems, including 'Ode to a Nightingale'. He also fell in love with the girl next door, Fanny Brawne. It was from this house that he travelled to Rome, where he died of tuberculosis aged just 25. Keats House has a busy schedule of annual family activities which can be found on the Events page of their website; these usually include an Egg Hunt at Easter and education and poetry workshops.

in summer. A path leads south up the hill and through dense woodland to one of north London's hidden pastoral gems, the **Hill Garden & Pergola** (Inverforth Close, off North End Way, NW3, tube: Golders Green or Hampstead). This secret Italianate arts and crafts garden was created between 1910 and 1925 by the most celebrated landscape architect of the Edwardian era, Thomas Hayton Mawson, for Unilever tycoon Lord Leverhulme; it was restored in the 1990s.

The Heath and its associated parks have, perhaps, the best sporting facilities of any London park, with an all-weather athletics track, cricket, football and rugby pitches, croquet lawns, an orienteering course, hard and grass tennis courts (and coaching) and a cross-country running route. Full details are on the website.

away is the equally impressive **Shri Swaminarayan Mandir** (105-119 Brentfield Rd, NW10 8LD, T020-8965 2651, mandir.org, tube: Neasden, Wembley Park, Stonebridge Park), Europe's first traditional Hindu temple. Next to the *mandir* is an intricately designed traditional wooden *haveli*, an exquisitely carved wooden mansion house, which is the only one to have been built anywhere in the world in the last 100 years. A total of 169 skilled craftsmen carried out the woodcarving at eight key sites throughout India over two years. Children seldom fail to be entranced by the buildings, which are unique in Britain, and there can be few better ways of getting them enthused about Hindu London. Note that men and women should not wear shorts and women should cover their arms when visiting the temples.

Go hunting in the forest

Epping Forest is the largest public open space in the London area, covering some 6000 acres of woodland and meadow between Manor Park in London and Epping in Essex. It is the wildest stretch of country in any British city and a great place for kids to romp around, wade through little streams, spot birds and butterflies or simply take a walk, cycle or horse ride. There are dozens of spots for a picnic, plenty of playgrounds and sports facilities,

and a handful of interesting historic sights, including **The Temple** (Wanstead Park, E11, T020-8989 7851, wansteadpark. org.uk, late Sep-late Mar Sat-Sun 1000-1500, late Mar-late Sep Sat-Sun 1200-1700), an 18th-century house set in classical gardens, with ornamental lakes, lawns and glades, and **Queen Elizabeth's Hunting Lodge** (T020-8529 6681, summer Wed-Sun 1000-1700, winter Fri-Sun 1000-1700), a unique Tudor house built for spectators on the royal hunt in Henry VIII's reign. Guests could simply watch the king in action, or participate by shooting crossbows at passing deer from the upper floors. After the hunt, guests were entertained with lavish feasts of spit-roast venison and barrels of mead and ale. Today the building is a small museum, with displays that include a medieval kitchen and an area where children can dress up in Tudor costumes. There are great views from the upper floors over the forest and the grassy meadows of Chingford Plain. A new visitor centre next door provides information about the forest, including details of wildlife. There is also a Forest Visitor Centre in **High Beach** (T020-8508 0028, cityoflondon.gov.uk, late Sep-late Mar daily 1000-1500, late Mar-late Sep daily 1000-1700, tube: Loughton or Buckhurst Hill), with leaflets and guides, a schedule of seasonal activities and a small gift shop.

Big days out

London Zoo

Regent's Park, London NW1, 19 Feb-Mar daily 1000-1630, Mar-Jul 1000-1730, Jul-Sep 1000-1800, Sep-Oct 1000-1730, Nov-19 Feb 1000-1600, extended opening on select days (see website), £17.60 adult, £13.70 child, under 3s free, tube: Camden Town or Regent's Park.

Over the last 30 years London Zoo has undergone a sometimes painful transition from an old-fashioned Victorian animal collection to a modern zoo, whose primary focus is animal conservation and species preservation. Animals are now kept in enclosures that mimic a natural habitat. Gorillas no longer pace up and down looking distressed and bored; they sit on a £5.3 million island surrounded by a moat or rest in glass-fronted enclosures, separated from onlookers by a few centimetres of toughened glass. The zoo is constantly being improved and upgraded. In May 2011 the penguins will move from their famous Grade I-listed pool (designed by Russian émigré Berthold Lubetkin) to a new pad: an artificial beach, complete with lapping waves. Other recent additions include a tropical bird walk-through, called the Blackburn Pavilion, and a children's zoo. In the Animal Adventure exhibit, children can clamber through tunnels to peer at underground aardvarks and meerkats in their burrows. They swing and climb alongside coatimundis in the Treetop zone, get wet and wild in artificial streams in the Splash zone (drying off in a teepee while being read a story), and pet kune-kune pigs in the Touch zone. The BUGS exhibit allows thrilled children to get uncomfortably close to giant hissing cockroaches, orb spiders and a locust swarm, and to see directly into a working honeybee hive and a leaf-cutter ant nest. The Aquarium is one of the largest in Britain, with superb displays showcasing Amazon species (including rare freshwater stingrays) and excellent education tanks containing British freshwater and marine life.

Despite all these innovations, parts of the zoo remain old-fashioned, some delightfully so: check out the Reptile House made famous by Harry Potter, or the original 1828 Clock Tower designed by zoo founder, Decimus Burton, and the deliciously dated modernist concrete Casson pavilion, built for elephants and rhinos, who have long since moved to more commodious quarters. Even in the upgraded areas, there is no avoiding the plain fact that London Zoo covers a small area, even by metropolitan standards: just over 37 acres, as compared to 250 acres for the Bronx Zoo in New York, for instance. This means that the 700-

plus species feel rather crowded-in and, even though the zoo is caring and conservation-conscious, some of the big mammals like the cats, zebras and giraffes look a little bored with their plain and modestly sized surrounds.

The zoo can be very busy at weekends in the summer

I like going to London Zoo because the monkeys do funny tricks, the fish in the aquarium look really weird and when they come to the glass they make me laugh.

Melissa, aged seven

months; visit on a weekday morning for the smallest crowds. And, avoid the restaurants, which are poor quality and poor value; there are better options in nearby Camden.

More family favourites

Highgate Cemetery
Swain's Lane, N6 6PJ, T020-8340 1834, highgate-cemetery.org. East Cemetery Mar-Oct daily 1000-1630, Nov-Feb daily 1000-1600. £3, under 16s free.

West Cemetery guided tours only, £7, £3 child, no under 8s. Tube: Archway. With its vine-encrusted mausoleums, spooky dark tombs and thick woods, Highgate Cemetery looks like a set from a gothic vampire movie. Indeed a vampire is said to have stalked London from here in the 1970s; it was hunted by two exorcists whose attempts to dispel the spirit from the tombs were reported on ITV. The cemetery is still said to be haunted by a host of ghosts. Many historical heroes and villains are buried here, most famously Karl Marx (whose tomb lies in the East Cemetery) and also writers George Eliot and Jacob Bronowski, Adam Worth (the inspiration for Professor Moriarty) and Malcolm McClaren. The cemetery can easily be visited in conjunction with neighbouring Waterlow Park (see page 90).

Jewish Museum
Raymond Burton House, 129-131 Albert St, NW1 7NB, T020-7284 7384, jewishmuseum.org.uk. Sun-Thu 1000-1700, Fri 1000-1400, £7, £6 concessions, £3 child, under 5s free. Tube: Camden Town.
This wonderful small museum reopened in 2010 after a £10 million investment, with spanking new galleries in a bright open-plan space in Camden. It's a great place for kids and adults alike to explore Jewish heritage, both in general and through the story of Jewish communities in Britain. There have been Jews in London for many centuries; the museum traces their history through early artefacts, including a ritual medieval milk bath (only discovered in 2001), a stunning 17th-century Venetian Ark found in Chillingham Castle in 1932. There's an evocation of a turn-of-the-19th-century Jewish East End street (with sights and sounds), displays telling stories of refugees from Nazism (who included

Football crazy?

North London is home to two big London football clubs: **Tottenham Hotspur** (spurs.co.uk), based at White Hart Lane in Tottenham, and **Arsenal** (arsenal.com) at the Emirates Stadium in Highbury. It's also the location of the sport's premier venue, **Wembley Stadium** (Wembley, HA9 0WS, T020-8795 9660, wembleystadium.com, tube: Wembley Park, Wembley Central, rail: Wembley Stadium). Tickets for games should be bought a season in advance. Tottenham have occasional tours of the pitch, tunnel and changing rooms at White Hart Lane (book ahead through the website). Arsenal has a club museum (Mon-Sat 1000-1800, Sun 1000 1700, £6, £3 under 16s, under 5s free), with signed shirts, cups medals and a full history of the club. There are also daily tours of Wembley Stadium (£15, £8 child, £38 family), except during matches and other events. The **Elms Football Academy** (Pynnacles Close, Stanmore, HA7 4AF, T020-8954 8787, theelms. co.uk, tube: Stanmore) has weekend coaching classes.

10,000 unaccompanied children) and profiles of influential figures like Benjamin Disraeli. Kids can knead bread, taste soup, sing karaoke songs in Yiddish and, in the Educational Space, they can handle ritual objects and enjoy creative craft activities, including traditional glass painting and candle making.

London Canal Museum

12-13 New Wharf Rd, N1, T020-7713 0836, canalmuseum.org.uk, Tue-Sun 1000-1630 (until 1930 on 1st Thu of month), £4, £3 concessions, £2 child, under 4s free. Tube/rail: King's Cross St Pancras.

For a taste of what life was like aboard a Victorian barge boat, visit this former Victorian ice storage warehouse by the water's edge near King's Cross. The museum is spread over two floors and is packed with fascinating items, from old boats decked out in original furniture to the folk paintings that once adorned them. There are Victorian costumes and Heath Robinson contraptions used in the ice trade. The museum also preserves London's only remaining ice well – a 12 m-deep hole in the ground in which the Victorians stored hundreds of tons of ice, which was supplied to London businesses all year round. The museum overlooks the Battlebridge Basin, which is packed with colourful residential barges and boats, including the

Curtain call

North London has more than its fair share of children's theatres and performance spaces. These include the **Chicken Shed** (290 Chase Side, N14 4PE, T020-8351 6161, chickenshed.org.uk, tube: Cockfosters), which has performances on Fridays and Saturdays acted by children aged from toddler to teenage. The **Artsdepot** (5 Nether St, N12 0GA, T020-8369 5454, artsdepot.co.uk, tube: West Finchley) has performances on Saturdays. **Jackson's Lane** (269A Archway Rd, N6 5AA, jacksonslane.org.uk, tube: Highgate), which is housed in a large Victorian former church, has performances from children's theatre companies most Sunday afternoons. **The Little Angel Theatre** (14 Dagmar Passage, N1 2DN, T020-7226 1787, littleangeltheatre.com, tube: Angel), tucked down an alleyway off busy Upper Street in Islington calls itself 'the home of British Puppetry'. The theatre puts on up to five children's productions every year alongside a range of visiting shows, with performances from Wednesday to Sunday (times vary) and additional shows on weekdays during school holidays. There are also puppetry courses for kids.

From May to September, **Regent's Park Open Air Theatre Company** (NW1, T0844-826 4242, openairtheatre.org, tickets from £5) performs drama under the stars in a pretty amphitheatre, surrounded by trees, in the heart of Regent's Park (see page 88). The repertoire includes family classics like *The Beggar's Opera* and Shakespeare re-imagined for children of six years old and over. The **Garden Suburbs Open Air Theatre** (T020-7723 6609, gardensuburbtheatre.org.uk, tube: Golders Green or East Finchley and bus 102) is a charming, tiny open-air theatre sitting in a little grove in a remnant of the Middlesex forest. The former amateur theatre company stages children's theatre productions most summers.

museum's *Bantam IV* tug. A little gift shop sells lovely wooden models of canal boats, soft toys, books and colourful tea towels.

Lord's Cricket Ground MCC Museum

St John's Wood, NW8 8QN, T020-7616 8595, lords.org. Apr-Oct Mon-Fri 1000-1700, Nov-Mar Mon-Thu 1130-1700, Fri 1130-1600. £7.50, £5 concessions. Tube: St John's Wood. The world's oldest sports museum houses a panoply of cricketing artefacts, from Victorian bats and balls to

modern trophies and the first Ashes urn, presented in 1882. The best way to see the museum is on a guided tour (£15, £9 concessions), which also takes in the ground, the MCC committee room and the commentary boxes.

Madame Tussaud's

Marylebone Rd, NW1 5LR, madametussauds.com. Mon-Fri 0930-1730, Sat-Sun 0900-1800 (extended hours during school holidays). £28.80, £24.60 child (discounts online). Tube: Baker Street.

Out & about North London

Come to the world's most famous waxworks museum forewarned and forearmed. Although the models are eerily realistic and the museum keeps bang up to date with celebrity fashion, many visitors find it overpriced, overcrowded and over-hyped. Visits can be particularly frustrating with young children. In the summer season waits of over an hour are usual and, once inside, you can expect to be jostled and shoved around, and to queue yet more for photos of you next to the most fashionable dummies. Prams and buggies are not permitted inside, so you'll have to carry babies and toddlers, and there are hidden extra charges for posing with 'special' exhibits. The museum is divided into galleries. At the 'A-List Party' you can pose with effigies of Nicole Kidman, Brad and Angelina, Orlando Bloom

and Leonardo DiCaprio, amongst others, and be part of a photo shoot with Kate Moss. 'Premiere Night' offers similar, with more established celebrities, including Harrison Ford (as Indiana Jones), Spiderman and Shrek. 'Music Megastars' has the likes of JLo, Beyoncé, Justin Timberlake and Cheryl Cole, and the 'Sports Zone' has a bemused-looking Lewis Hamilton, David Beckham, Sachin Tendulka and Cristiano Ronaldo. There's royalty too, although Diana, Princess of Wales is tucked away downstairs next to Liza Minelli rather than with the royal family. A special Chamber of Horrors exhibit for older kids only is modelled on the London dungeons and has actors posing as waxworks leaping out at visitors to make them scream.

Royal Airforce Museum
Grahame Park Way, NW19 5LL, T020-8205 2266, rafmuseum.org.uk. Daily

1000-1800, closed 24-26 Dec and 1 Jan. Free. Tube: Colindale.
This large museum housed in the former RAF aerodrome in Colindale preserves more than 100 aircraft from all over the world, from the earliest flying machines to modern fighter jets. It's immensely popular with kids of all ages, who can sit in cockpits and pretend to be a pilot, or learn about the story of flight through engaging, modern interactive video displays. The aircraft themselves hang from the ceiling in the vast main gallery. They include some very early pioneer machines like the 1909 Bleriot (named after the Frenchman who became the first person to cross the English Channel by plane on the 25 July 1909) and the Sopwith Camel which was used on the Western Front in 1917. These sit alongside Spitfires and Avro Lancaster bombers and the latest modern-day jets and military aircraft, including the Eurofighter Typhoon. There are also twin-rotor Boeing Chinook helicopters, Harriers, De Havilland Mosquitoes, Lightings, Britannias and Mustangs and a host of lethal weapons, including all manner of bombs and missiles. The Aeronauts Interactive exhibit

Royal Airforce Museum.

Sherlock Holmes Museum.

(many of whose activities are not suitable for under 10s) has more than 40 hands-on activities, including real and simulated cockpits to sit in, packets to drop on parachutes, pulling, pushing, blowing, bashing and balancing experiments and even a flight simulator (the only exhibit in the museum which is not free). The museum has an excellent café where you can eat sandwiches and sip hot chocolate under the wings of fighters and bombers, and a small gift shop.

Sherlock Holmes Museum
221B Baker St, NW1 6XE, T020-7224 3688, sherlock-holmes.co.uk.

Daily 0930-1800. £6, £4 child. Tube: Baker Street.

This museum offers a lovingly created version of the home the fictional detective shared with Dr Watson on Baker Street. It's a delight for all Holmes fans, young and old. A strict-looking Edwardian policeman, in a turn-of-the-19th-century uniform quizzes visitors as they arrive at the front door and each room of the four-storey townhouse reproduces details from Conan Doyle's short stories and novels. The sitting room comes complete with stately armchairs, Holmes' violin, Persian slippers, forensic equipment and

detective paraphernalia. There's also a 'VR' on the wall pocked with bullet holes – a reference to *The Musgrave Ritual*, in which Holmes uses the living room for target practice. The downstairs shop sells all manner of things related to the detective, from DVDs of television adaptations to mugs and deerstalker hats.

Action stations

Canal boating
The **London Waterbus Company** (58 Camden Lock Pl, London NW1, T020-7482 2550, londonwaterbus.com, single 50 mins, £6.70, £5.50 child, return

110 mins, £9.70, £7.70 child) runs short cruises along the Regent's Canal in close-sided barges, leaving from Brownings Pool in Little Venice or Camden Lock and running through the long, dark and spooky Maida Vale tunnel, past Regent's Park and London Zoo. The barges can also pick up at London Zoo for a slightly reduced fee. For the timetable, consult the website. **Jason's** (opposite 42 Blomfield Rd, W9, jasons.co.uk, Apr-Nov only, single £8, £7 child, return £9, £8 child) runs a similar service thrice daily in summer on an open-sided 100-year-old canal boat. The **London Canal Museum** (see page 97) also offers a number of boat trips, including a night-time Hallowe'en Experience cruise in a specially decorated boat, which takes in the 200-year-old Islington tunnel.

Riding
Kentish Town City Farm
(ktcityfarm.org.uk; see page 91) offers pony rides for children over four years old every Saturday at 1330 (£1) and group riding sessions during the summer holidays on Thursday and Friday afternoons (book ahead). Staff at the **Epping Forest Visitor Centre** (see page 94) can recommend stables for pony riding in the forest.

Swimming
Children under eight are not permitted at the famous open-

Wildlife watch

North London's parks are rich in wildlife. Visiting as early as possible (ideally close to dawn) during the week, when the parks are invariably empty of both people and dogs, will reveal them to be as busy with birds, small mammals and reptiles as a countryside wood. Foxes, hedgehogs, grey squirrels, rabbits, voles, water rats, weasels, grass snakes, slow worms, badgers and hares can all be found in Hampstead Heath, Alexandra Park and Highgate and Queen's Woods, together with five bat species, more than 70 bird species, 180 species of moth, 12 species of butterfly and 80 species of spider. The Heath, Highgate and Queen's Woods and Abney Park Cemetery are very rich in birdlife. The Heath is good for finches, tits and warblers, as well as common garden birds, like blackbirds, jays and magpies. Look out for the very rare white robin with a red breast near the tennis courts on Parliament Hill and in the cherry trees near William Ellis School. Three species of British woodpecker can be seen in north London's parks, including the large green woodpecker. Kingfishers, reed and sedge warblers and water rails breed in the Hampstead Ponds, alongside familiar coot and moorhens and many duck species. Parliament Hill is a great spot to see birds moving from one part of the city to another, especially early in the morning, when, if you are lucky, you can see rare birds of prey, including hobby, honey buzzard and osprey, as well as the far more numerous passerines. Sparrowhawk and tawny owls breed annually on Hampstead Heath, in Highgate Wood and at the Abney Park Cemetery. The parks also have foreign species. Flocks of chirruping rose-ringed parakeets (which are endemic in India) are a common sight on Hampstead Heath and in Abney Park Cemetery. And the ultra-shy Labrador-sized muntjac or barking deer are present in all the larger parks.

For more information see the park websites and those of the **London Natural History Society** (lnhs.org.uk), **RSPB** (rspb.org.uk), the **London Birders Club** (londonbirders.wikia.com) and the **London Wildlife Trust** (wildlondon. org.uk), all of whom run children's activity programmes throughout London. Also see Epping Forest, page 94.

air Hampstead Heath Ponds (NW5 1QR, T020-7485 3873, cityoflondon.gov.uk, daily, times vary, £2, £1 concessions, rail: Gospel Oak); under 16s must be accompanied and may be asked to pass a swimming test. However, children of all ages can swim in the 60-m unheated **Parliament Hill Lido & Paddling Pool** (Gordon House Rd, T020-7485 3873, May to mid-Sep daily 0700-0930 and 1000-1830, mid-Sep to Apr daily 0700-0030, £2, rail: Gospel Oak), one of a handful of all-year-round outdoor swimming venues in London. (There are additional summer evening sessions for adults only on Mon, Thu and Fri.) An adjacent café serves piping hot chocolate, in summer only.

Walking tours
The **London Canal Museum** (T020-7713 0836, canalmuseum. org.uk, phone for schedule, £5, £4 child) organizes two guided walks along the Regent's Canal. Both start from the museum, cutting through streets to join the Regent's Canal at Caledonian Road, then following the towpath west past towering Victorian gas stations and abandoned warehouses to St Pancras Lock, and then either to Camden or up a huge Victorian watertower that once provided water for steam trains at St Pancras station. There are wonderful views of the city from the top which make the walk worthwhile, even for kids who have no interest at all in canals and barges.

Park life

North London has plenty of parks and green spaces, many of them with semi-wild woodland areas. In addition to elegant Regent's Park (see page 88), inspiring Hampstead Heath (see page 92) and sprawling Epping Forest (see page 94), try some of the following for walks, picnics, wildlife-watching or simply playing to the sound of birdsong.

Alexandra Park (Alexandra Palace Way, N22, T020-8365 2121, alexandrapalace.com, tube: Wood Green and then bus W3). Families come to Alexandra Park for the superb views of the city, the delightful shady walks and Alexandra Palace, the gargantuan Victorian hall which hosted the second Great Exhibition of 1862. The palace was once a headquarters for the BBC, who made their first public broadcast from here, but is now an events and concert

My favourite place in London is the ice skating rink in Alexandra Palace. I love to watch the gleaming, crystal ice shine. I adore slipping and sliding on the ice because it always makes my friends laugh and I like making them laugh. The best thing is when I stand on the side and watch people skid.

Noa, aged 10

space and an all-year-round ice rink. The park sprawls at its feet, in lawns, rose gardens and little copses, and stretches behind in playgrounds, skateboard parks and a pleasant little boating lake overlooked by a rustic café.

Camley Street Natural Park (12 Camley St, N1, T020-7833 2311, wildlondon.org.uk, daily 1000-1700) is a two-acre reserve set in a former steam engine coal yard on the banks of the Regent's Canal, right next to the new St Pancras Eurostar terminus. It's a beautiful spot, set aside as wild land, marsh, reed beds, woodland and meadow, and filled with water birds including reed warblers, kingfishers and buntings. Kids can see stag beetles, nesting birds, herons and common frogs, play with the two resident rabbits, Coco and Merlin, or simply have a snack and breather after the queues and chaos of nearby Madame Tussaud's.

Finsbury and Clissold parks (haringey.gov.uk, clissoldpark. com, tube: Finsbury Park or Manor House). Were it not in so disreputable a neighbourhood, **Finsbury Park** would be one of the most enchanting public spaces in all London. It is a perfect blend of formal gardens, common ground and shady woodland, broken by ornamental ponds, cafés and little art galleries, with a view of

the City of London hovering at the horizon. There are no end of sporting facilities and the park also hosts a number of big summer concerts and events. Facilities for kids are excellent; there's a (dog-free) play area with an exciting water feature, designed by children, and a big skate park. **Clissold Park**, 500 m southeast, is equally great for kids, with a small zoo, aviary and butterfly farm, a large ornamental pond, grazing deer and a pretty little stream busy with waterfowl. Both parks have excellent playgrounds.

Gladstone Park (Kendal Rd, NW10, tube: Dollis Hill). This forgotten North London park has been delighting those who chance upon it since it was a private garden of the Finch family of Dollis Hill House in the 19th century. When he visited in 1900, Mark Twain wrote: "I have never seen any place that was so satisfactorily situated, with its noble trees and stretch of country, and everything that went to make life delightful, and all within a biscuit's throw of the metropolis of the world." Willesden council bought the land in 1900 and named the gardens after William Gladstone, who had been a frequent visitor. The once magnificent house has suffered two arson attacks and, for now, is boarded-up and closed but the park remains as delightful as it was in the great

prime minister's time. Its secret corners and avenues, leading to a hedged rose garden, a hidden duck pond, an arboretum and a rustic playground, make it especially beloved of children. There are also tennis courts, an art gallery, a pretty little café tucked at the back of the rose garden, and adult and junior sports pitches.

Highgate Wood and **Queen's Wood** (T020-8444 6129, cityoflondon.gov.uk, daily 0730-sunset, free, tube: Highgate) cover some 70 acres of principally oak and hornbeam woodland, cut by paths (which are buggy-friendly) and interspersed with lawns and wide open spaces. There are a series of playgrounds and the wood is home to much wildlife (see page 101). A list of species and seasonal events is available on the website.

Other parks in north London include **Highbury Fields** (highburyfieldsassociation.org, tube: Highbury & Islington) in Islington, which has one of the city's best adventure playgrounds, and **Queen's Park** (cityoflondon.gov.uk, tube: Brondesbury Park), which is justifiably famous for its spring flowers and which has a lovely pet's corner with pygmy goats.

Boating lake in Alexandra Park.

Contents

South London

Battersea Power Station.

You must

❶ Watch rare wildlife and birds at the Wetland Centre.

❷ Dally with the dinosaurs in Crystal Palace Park.

❸ Marvel at the musical instruments in the Horniman Museum.

❹ Picnic in the park at Battersea, Clapham or Dulwich.

❺ Admire the Peace Pagoda in Battersea Park.

❻ Stroke a Shetland pony in Battersea Park children's zoo.

❼ Discover the costs of war at the Imperial War Museum.

❽ Admire the art in the Dulwich Picture Gallery.

❾ Wander the river bank along the Thames Path.

❿ Skate away the day at the Streatham Ice Rink.

South London traditionally begins immediately across the river from Westminster and the City, but the city centre has long since spread across the bridges to claim a large swathe of the region for itself, so you'll find the London Eye, Tower Bridge and the sights between them on the South Bank in our Central London chapter.

For the purposes of this book, South London incorporates the borough of Lambeth, south of Waterloo, home to the **Imperial War Museum**, which mixes Boys' Own paraphernalia with considered and thought-provoking exhibits on the cost of war. Lambeth's neighbour Southwark begins at the Thames but runs far south through well-to-do Dulwich and Forest Hill, where kids can run about and play in large and leafy **Dulwich Park** and explore the delightful child-friendly and crowd-free collections at the **Dulwich Picture Gallery** and **Horniman Museum**. The borough of Wandsworth stretches west through **Battersea**, with its famous power station and lovely riverside park, and on to Putney and Barnes, where children come to visit the **Wildfowl & Wetlands Trust Centre**, the largest urban wetland reserve in Europe. Note that we include Greenwich (south of the river to the east) and Wimbledon and Richmond (to the west) in our East and West London chapters, respectively.

Out & about South London

Fun & free

Be at peace in the park

Battersea Park (SW11, batterseapark.org, daily 0800-dusk, rail: Battersea Park or Queenstown Road) is one of the few south London parks worth making a special trip for. It has lovely views over the river, an adventure playground, ponds filled with terrapins, a boating lake, gardens, woodland and brightly lit fountains. Most interesting for kids are the **children's zoo** (T020-7924 5826, batterseaparkzoo.co.uk, summer daily 1000-1730, winter daily 1000-1630, £7.50, £6 child,

under 2s free) and the exotic **Peace Pagoda**. The former lets kids get up close to ring-tailed lemurs, meerkats, Shetland ponies, brown capuchin monkeys and many other animals. The latter sits serenely overlooking the Thames at the north of the park. It is the largest Buddhist monument in London and was given to the people of London by the Japanese Nipponzan Myohoji Buddhist Order as part of the Greater London Council Peace Year in 1984. The Pagoda has four large gilded sculptures of the Buddha on each of its four sides, each showing a different

mudra (hand gesture that refers to some event in the life of the Buddha or to a particular spiritual truth). If you're visiting in November, note that the park has one of the best firework displays in the city on Bonfire Night (see page 15).

Meet the dinosaurs

Crystal Palace Park (Thicket Rd, SE20, T020-8313 4471, rail: Crystal Palace) vies with Battersea Park as the best in south London for kids. The park was the site of the 1851 Great Exhibition, for which the giant crystal palace was built. Today,

It's a dog's life

Children pining for a puppy should take a visit to Battersea London's famous home for canine and feline waifs (battersea.org.uk). It was founded in 1860 by Mary Tealby who was distressed by the number of strays in London's streets and set up kennels for them in Holloway. The home moved to its present Battersea location in 1871 and started taking in cats in 1883. The strays touched the hearts of a host of famous Londoners, including Charles Dickens and Queen Victoria; the home has had royal patronage since 1884. By 1909 it was running two lorries and six horse-drawn carriages to collect strays and, in 1911, it first started collecting from the police. Many Battersea dogs have played an important role in British history: pulling Shackleton's sledges across Antarctica in 1914 and serving in both World Wars. Airedale Jack, a Battersea dog, was awarded an animal VC for delivering a vital plea for reinforcements on the frontline in France in 1918; he died in the attempt but his battalion was saved. Casual visitors to the home are as welcome as those looking for a pet.

Top left: Peace Pagoda. Left: Chelsea Bridge.
Above: Black swan in Battersea Park.

only a few relics of the palace remain: the steps which led to the building and a concrete sphinx which stood sentinel beside them. The biggest draw, though, are the 33 Victorian dinosaurs built three years later by Benjamin Waterhouse Hawkins. They were the first ever life-sized replicas of dinosaurs and though they have long been discredited as biologically inaccurate by experts, they look wonderfully animated and monstrous, nonetheless. Hawkins was a natural history artist and sculptor who contributed illustrations to Darwin's *The Zoology of the Voyage of HMS Beagle*. He modelled the dinosaur sculptures under the supervision of Professor Richard Owen, who coined the word 'dinosaur', and based his likenesses on fossils. But children who know their prehistoric reptiles will spot that the iguanodon's vicious thumb-spike is anatomically misplaced, appearing as a horn on Hawkins' models. The park also boasts the largest maze in London, a boating lake, a children's farm, a playground, an outdoor concert stage and woods and fields to run about in.

Dinosaurs in Crystal Palace Park.

Park life: South London

South London is not as well-endowed with green spaces as the north but there are still some large, attractive green spaces and some extensive areas of semi-wilderness on the city's fringes. Few are visited, so it's easy to find acres in which to roam free within easy access of public transport, especially during the week. For Battersea Park and Crystal Palace Park, see pages 108–110.

Brockwell Park (lambeth.gov.uk, tube: Brixton or rail: Herne Hill) is a large park between Herne Hill and Brixton. It has one of the few purpose-built BMX circuits in London as well as a popular outdoor swimming pool, the Brockwell Lido (see page 117). There are also Australian rules football pitches, cricket nets, football pitches, tennis courts and a basketball court.

Clapham Common (lambeth.gov.uk, tube: Clapham Common or Clapham South) is a large rather unsightly grassy meadow, sparsely patched with trees and three large ponds, all of which were former gravel pits. The largest of these is a popular spot for model boating. The common has an all-weather skateboarding and recreation area (which is a great spot to drive radio-controlled cars), tennis courts, sports pitches and two poorly equipped playgrounds.

Dulwich Park (southwark.gov.uk, rail: East Dulwich) covers some 72 acres of grassland, meadow, woods and formal gardens. It has one of the largest and best-equipped children's playgrounds in south London, a boating lake, bike hire facilities and an activity centre in the Francis Peek building.

Southwark Park (southwark.gov.uk, tube: Canada Water), near the river in Bermondsey, is great for sports, with tennis courts, cricket and football pitches and an athletics track. It also has a lovely little butterfly farm, which is popular with mums and toddlers, a boating lake, rose gardens, a small art gallery and a decent playground.

Sydenham Hill Wood (rail: Forest Hill or Sydenham Hill) is a remnant of old oak and beech woodland dotted with sculptures by local artists and with its own (fake) ruined monastery. Nearby **Dawson's Hill** (dawsonshill. org.uk) has extensive meadows and woodlands and, perhaps, the best city centre views in south London. A children's nature trail can be downloaded from the website.

Don't miss Horniman Museum

100 London Rd, Forest Hill, SE23 3PQ, T020-8699 1872, horniman.ac.uk. House daily 1020-1730, closed 24-26 Dec. Gardens Mon-Sat 0730-sunset. Free, except for aquarium £2.50. Rail: Forest Hill.

Many of London's museums can be a little overwhelming for children; there is simply so much to see that small minds and short attention spans easily overdose. The big museums can be overcrowded too – especially at weekends and in the summer months – and short on rest space. Not so the Horniman. This is the perfect first museum for kids: it has a little bit of almost everything in bite-sized chunks, is rarely crowded, is easily digestible in an hour or two and has plenty of kids' activities on offer. It's in a great location too, housed in a gloriously quirky Edwardian building sitting in the middle of a pretty, wooded 16-acre park that is brilliant with brightly coloured flowers in spring and summer and offers some of the best views in south London. Note that pushchairs

are not permitted in the galleries but there is a spacious buggy park on the lower ground floor.

The museum was founded by Victorian tea trader and collector, Frederick Horniman, who became fascinated by foreign travel and all things exotic after leaving Britain for the first time aged 60. Horniman had his staff bring back curios from around the world for the family collection and acquired still more though the auction houses of London. When his collection outgrew the family home, the collector commissioned arts and crafts architect Charles Harrison Townsend to design a new museum. The resulting building was as strange as the collection itself: a fusion of arts and crafts, art nouveau and Saxon English, fronted by a brightly coloured mosaic frieze and dominated by a splendid castellated sandstone clocktower. The museum opened in 1901 and was "dedicated with the surrounding land as a free gift to the people of London by Frederick Horniman forever

for their recreation, instruction and enjoyment."

There are five main galleries in the Horniman. **African Worlds** was the first permanent exhibition in Britain to profile African art and culture, and remains one of the best. Highlights include a series of brilliantly coloured masks, Egyptian mummies and religious altars from Benin, Brazil and Haiti. There's also a huge metal globe which kids love to set spinning at a furious pace. The **Music Gallery** traces the history of a panoply of musical instruments: 1600 drums, concertinas, clarinets, keyboards, bassoons, trumpets, trombones, harps and violins and their ancestors are housed in giant glass cases lining the walls. Look out for one of the first saxophones, invented in 1841 by Belgian, Adolphe Sax. At the far end is a performance and demonstration area, where kids can listen to or look at a rare instrument from the collection. The **Centenary Gallery** houses a mish-mash of costumes, bizarre ritual objects (many from Papua New Guinea) and Victoriana from Horniman's collection. Oddest of all is the shockingly realistic Japanese merman – half monkey, half fish – which is so perfectly grafted together that it fooled sailors for many years into believing that such creatures existed in Asia. The **Natural History Galleries** are a mix of environmentalism and

late Victorian collector-mania with hundreds of models and stuffed creatures, many of them made extinct by man. The most poignant, perhaps, is the passenger pigeon, which was systematically, commercially slaughtered to extinction in North America in the late 19th century. A pair of what was once the most common bird on the planet now perches for eternity on a varnished twig at the entrance to the gallery. The basement of the museum is home to a pocket-sized but charming **aquarium**, whose exhibits are dominated by British fresh and saltwater fish and invertebrates but also include tanks recreating a South American rainforest river, a Fijian reef and a Caribbean mangrove wetland. There is a touch tank where children can get their hands on crabs and starfish. The museum also has two smaller hands-on galleries specifically for children. At **Nature Base** kids can touch objects and live animals, such as the harvest mouse and the Horniman beetle, named after the museum's founder. The **Hands on Base** allows children to touch hundreds of objects from the collection as well as draw, scribble and play a variety of games. There are also activity trails for all the galleries. The bright, healthy café, which serves attractively priced food is a great spot for lunch or tea after a tour of the museum.

Out & about South London

Big days out

WWT London Wetland Centre

Queen Elizabeth's Walk, Barnes, SW13 9WT, T020-8409 4400, wwt.org.uk. Winter daily 0930-1700 (last entry 1600), summer daily 0930-1800 (last entry 1700). £10.55, £7.85 concessions, £5.85 child, under 4s free (these prices include Gift Aid donation). Tours daily 1100 and 1400, free. Walk with a warden Sat-Sun 1200, free. Tube: Hammersmith then bus 283, rail: Barnes or Barnes Bridge then bus.

This 104-acre private reserve next to the Thames between Putney and Barnes is one of the best urban wildlife sites in Europe and one of only a handful of wetland projects in a capital city worldwide. There is no better place in London for children to get a taste of the wild and see rare British birds in a natural environment. There are 180 species here, including kingfishers, bitterns and water rails, alongside rare mammals like water voles, reptiles including grass snakes, most of Britain's amphibians and dozens of species of butterfly and moth. The park is a series of lakes, flooded meadows and marshlands gathered around a large main lake and linked together by buggy- and wheelchair-friendly walkways. World Wetlands, an area of the centre, has waterbirds from around the planet, including New Zealand black swans, endangered laysan teals and white-faced whistling ducks; you can help to feed them at 1500 daily. Wildside is a series of flower-filled meadows joined by little paths and dotted with frog-filled ponds. The reedbeds attract bitterns, warblers and ultra-rare bearded tits, while the main lake is where the largest flocks gather. There are hides all over the wetland from which children can watch wildlife under camouflage, a viewing tower with great panoramic views, a walk-through bat house and a duck-feeding pond. Children may be most excited by the Pond Zone, which allows them to get their hands on snails, rat-tailed maggots and tadpoles, and the Explore Zone,

Grey heron.

where they can whip down zip lines, scurry through giant water vole tunnels, climb boulder walls and get wet and dirty under a series of water exhibits (closed during winter). The free daily tours begin and end at the Visitor Centre, which has a wealth of information for kids, with activity trails and an interactive Discovery Centre that teaches children about the animals and plants they'll see in the reserve. There's also a good shop selling wildlife gifts and books, and a semi-al fresco café.

More family favourites

Dulwich Picture Gallery

Gallery Rd, Dulwich SE21, T020-8693 5254, dulwichpicturegallery.org.uk. Tue-Fri 1000-1700, Sat-Sun 1100-1700, closed 25-26 Dec and 1 Jan. £5, children free. Guided tours Sat-Sun 1500. Free. Rail: West Dulwich or North Dulwich.

This small, stout brick building with a cherry red interior is to art galleries what the Horniman (see page 112) is to museums – presenting a splendid collection of old master paintings in a child-friendly portion. They include van Dyck and Rubens, whose fat ladies dominate the Flemish room, Poussin and Claude in the French room, Raphael and Piero di Cosimo in the Italian, and some fine English portraiture from Tudor times through to Thomas Gainsborough. Although formal portraiture and highly stylized

Going over the top in the Imperial War Museum.

themes from classical mythology are not an obvious draw for kids, the paintings offer illuminating glimpses of life in bygone centuries, from the elaborate costumes of the Tudor portraits to a sylvan, pastoral Europe shown in paintings like Watteau's *Le Plaisir du Bal*. And the building itself is a splendid piece of John Soane quirky neoclassicism with skylight domes casting a beautiful soft light over the galleries. There are lovely lawned gardens, coloured by daffodils and shaded by exotic 200-year-old trees, that are great for a picnic and host numerous open-air events. The gallery also has a café (0900-1700), with outdoor tables in summer and a children's menu.

Imperial War Museum
Lambeth Rd, SE1 6HZ, TEL, iwm. orq.uk. Daily 1000-1800 (closed 15, 24-26 Dec). Free apart from special exhibitions. Tube: Lambeth North. Although the Spitfires, Polaris missiles, tanks and assorted displays of modern armoury will delight soldier-loving boys of all ages, this museum of modern warfare is far from being as bloodthirsty as one might expect. Sections on trench warfare, the Blitz and rationing, and the five-storey extension added in 2000, which is devoted almost entirely to the horrors of the Holocaust, will have even the most gung-ho teen reflecting on the human cost of war. A huge clock counts the

number of lives lost in armed conflicts around the globe – currently standing at over 100 million – and a new gallery, Crimes Against Humanity, recounts some of the worst genocides in modern history, principally through a 30-minute documentary film. It's pretty harrowing stuff, and many of the displays are not suitable for younger children; the museum actively discourages visits to the Holocaust gallery for children under 14. That said, a number of other galleries will fascinate rather than horrify. The Secret War exhibit tells the story of British espionage, focusing principally on the development of MI5 and MI6. There are plenty of spooks' gadgets, including bottles of invisible ink used by German spies in the First World War, an original German Enigma cipher machine, codebooks, SOE sabotage devices and a secret radio used by MI6 agents during the Cold War. The Large Exhibits gallery in the main hall of the building has some spectacular large weapons and military gadgets, including an M4 Sherman tank, an Italian 'human torpedo' underwater craft, a Spitfire, a Focke-Wulf 190, a Mustang, a V2 rocket, an atomic bomb housing and the Polaris missile. The madness of war is further emphasized by displays telling the story of the building itself; until the First

The Thames Path

This foot and cycle path (nationaltrail.co.uk) runs pretty much the whole course of the Thames, from its source in the Cotswolds through the entire city (mostly on the south bank of the river) to the Thames Barrier near Greenwich. It's a great way to break the monotony of the tube, get some relatively fresh air and see a bit of the river and many of London's most famous sights. The most popular section of the path runs along the South Bank in Central London (see page 32). The rest of the route is much less busy and includes some wonderfully pretty stretches. With young children, try the section between the brightly painted **Chelsea Bridge** (rail: Battersea Park) and newly refurbished **Albert Bridge** (rail: Clapham Junction, then bus 50, 88, 155 or 345), which cuts through **Battersea Park** (see page 108) past the Peace Pagoda, with wonderful views of two of the river's prettiest bridges. It is an easy 30-minute walk. Between **Putney** and **Hammersmith bridges** (tube: Putney Bridge or Hammersmith) the path is almost rural and is open to cyclists as well as walkers. Follow the gravel trail through woodland busy with birds and past the **WWT Wetland Centre** (see page 114) before emerging next to some vast Victorian warehouses, which are now blocks of flats for the well-to-do. There are plenty of other long and short routes, all of which can be planned through the Thames Path website.

World War it was the notorious Bethlehem Royal Hospital for London's insane – 'Bedlam' itself. The museum has a strong mission to educate young visitors and hosts a number of events and workshops for families (see below).

Action stations

Activities & workshops

The **Imperial War Museum** (iwm. org.uk; see page 115) website has details of its busy calendar of seasonal events for children; most are free and do not require pre-booking. These include drama workshops, at which kids are invited to re-enact classic war stories, storytelling and a family introduction to the Holocaust, with talks, explanations and a guided visit to the gallery.

Dulwich Picture Gallery (dulwichpicturegallery.org.uk; see page 114) offers plenty for families. ArtPlay (Jan-May Sun 1400-1530, no need to book, free with gallery entrance or £2 child) is a drop-in art activity session on the first and last Sunday each month, at which children and their parents work on anything from bunting to block printing. Art in the Garden (Wed 1400-1530, £2 child), a programme of drop-in creative family workshops held in the gardens, runs in the summer holidays. There are also special events and family days advertised on the website.

Ice skating

Temporary winter ice rinks are erected outside many of the city's landmark sights, including the Tower of London, London Eye, Hampton Court and in the courtyard of Somerset House (see page 57), but the city has a mere handful of permanent ice rinks. **Streatham Ice Arena** (386 Streatham High Rd, SW16 6HT, T020-8769 7771, streathamicearena.co.uk, £5-7, discounts for children attending regularly, rail: Streatham or Streatham Common) is a full-sized rink, suitable for ice skating and ice hockey, and is a great place to have fun on the ice or to begin to learn properly to skate.

Swimming

In the summer, join the locals for a dip at **Brockwell Lido** (Brockwell Park, Dulwich Rd, SE24 0PA, T020-7274 3088, brockwell-lido.com, Jun-Aug Mon-Fri 0630-2000, Sat-Sun 1000-1800, May and Sep Mon-Fri 0630-1000 and 1600-2000, Sat-Sun 1000-1800), which also has health and fitness facilities and a café on site. **Tooting Bec Lido** (Tooting Bec Rd, SW16 1RU, T020-8871 7198, wandsworth. gov.uk, end May-end Aug daily 0600-2000, Sep daily 0600-1700, £5, £3.20 concessions, under 5s free) has one of the largest open-air pools in Europe, plus a paddling pool and a café.

Curtain call

The **Battersea Arts Centre** (Lavender Hill, SW11, T020-7223 2223, bac.org.uk, rail: Clapham Junction) has a good programme of kids' theatre and musicals, a great new café called the Bee's Knees filled with free activities and games and a daily programme of storytelling, music and workshops. The lovely art deco **Broadway** (Catford Broadway, London SE6, T020-8690 0002, broadwaytheatre. org.uk, rail: Catford Bridge) has a spread of children's matinee shows and stages one of the city's most popular pantomimes. The **Colour House** (Merton Abbey Mill, SW19, T020-8542 5511, colourhousetheatre.co.uk, tube: Colliers Wood or South Wimbledon) stages children's classics, like *Beauty and the Beast* and *Cinderella*, performed by children. The **Croydon Warehouse** (62 Dingwall Rd, Croydon, CR0 2NF, T020-8680 4060, warehousetheatre.co.uk, rail & tram: East Croydon) is a tiny theatre with kids' shows most Saturdays, touring shows for toddlers and a great little theatre school.

Wildlife activities

The **Wetlands Centre** (wwt.org. uk; see page 114) runs a regular programme of children's activities at weekends and during the holidays; for details, see the website.

Contents

West London

Hampton Court.

West London sprung up around a series of palaces, stately homes and royal hunting grounds, and vestiges of monarchy and aristocracy still dominate the region.

Grandest of all is the vast Tudor palace at **Hampton Court**, which is set in equally vast gardens, whose yew hedge maze is immensely popular with children. Henry VIII liked to hunt deer in adjacent **Bushy Park**, which is cut by delightful streams undisturbed enough to be watched over by kingfishers. Charles I preferred **Richmond Park**, which remains the largest Royal Park in London, a vast sweep of grassy meadows and woodlands that provide a home for wild animals including herds of red deer and thousands of feral parakeets. Next to Richmond are the **Royal Botanical Gardens** at Kew, preserving the world's largest and most famous collection of plants, in enormous glasshouses, shady woodlands and brilliantly blooming flower beds. Stately homes cluster between them: **Ham House**, with its colourful past and haunted corridors, **Syon House**, which has a tropical zoo in its grounds, and **Osterley** and **Gunnersbury**, which sit in lovely, lawned parks. The region is divided by the Thames which is sleepy and lined with verdant and semi-wooded banks for much of its west London length.

Out & about West London

Go deer-stalking

Children will have fun spotting the wildlife in the huge semi-wilderness of **Richmond Park** (royalparks.gov.uk). There are shire horses, badgers, foxes, muntjac and hedgehogs, plus 650 free-roaming red and fallow deer. Also look out for butterflies, moths, beetles and 144 species of bird. Begin explorations with the lovely woodland **Isabella Plantation**, which has streams and ponds, and one of the best playgrounds in west London at the Petersham Gate. And, for a break, head to **Pembroke Lodge** (T020-8940 8207, summer daily 1000-1730, winter daily 1000-

dusk), a handsome Georgian mansion in the middle of the park set in formal gardens with great views of London. It houses a good restaurant that caters for children, with high chairs and nappy-changing facilities.

Hampton Court Palace

East Molesy, KT8, T020-3166 6000, hrp.org.uk. Daily 1000-1630. £15.40, £7.70 child. Rail: Hampton Court. Hampton Court Palace is the finest Tudor building in Britain, overflowing with history and crammed with glorious paintings and royal treasures. There are so many rooms and so much to see that it can be

Park life: West London

Gunnersbury Park Museum.

London's west is gloriously green, with vast areas of semi-wilderness south of the river in Wimbledon and Richmond (see page 122) and a series of pretty, more formal parks on the north bank.

Holland Park (rbkc.gov.uk, tube: Holland Park or High Street Kensington) preserves 54 acres of gardens and woodland. It has an excellent children's play area, outdoor chess for kids and one of London's hidden delights: the formal Japanese Kyoto Garden. The park has a café and facilities for tennis, football, golf, cricket and netball.

Gunnersbury Park (Pope's Lane, W5, T0845-456 2796, hounslow. gov.uk, tube: Acton Town) is one of London's prettiest and is dominated by a splendid Regency mansion turned museum, with a small gallery devoted to old toys and

games and a lovely café with a view. There are playgrounds, extensive tracts of woodland, huge lawns, a romantic mid-18th-century temple and Italian garden overlooking a lake, creepy vine-encrusted ruins and bluebell woods which burst into flower in April.

The riverside parks are good spots for a picnic by the Thames. **Bishop's Park** (tube: Putney Bridge) is a long strip of green right next to the river beside Fulham FC's Craven Cottage football ground. It affords lovely views of Putney on the south bank and has a pretty walled garden, tennis courts and a play area with a paddling pool.

Duke's Meadows (rail: Chiswick) is a big grassy, riverside park with lots of football pitches and tennis courts, two playgrounds and great river views.

Further west, **Bushy Park** (royalparks.gov.uk, rail: Hampton Wick), right next to Hampton Court Palace, is one of London's biggest areas of grass and woodland at 1100 acres and was Henry VIII's former hunting ground. Bird and wildlife is extensive here, with herds of deer, a small colony of water voles, rabbit warrens and huge flocks of waterbirds and parakeets. It is the best place in London to see kingfishers (along the Longford river), swans and skylarks and there are wonderful views of the back façade of Hampton Court Palace along a formal rectangular lake. There's a large playground, model boating pond and a swimming pool, and you can have picnics here (they are prohibited in Hampton Court's grounds).

Hampton Court highlights

★ Get lost in the maze.

★ Search for royal phantoms on the Kids' Ghost Trail.

★ Rush around the acres of gardens.

★ Marvel at the weapons hanging on the walls in the King's Guard Chamber.

★ Look for fish and frogspawn in the fountains and ponds.

★ Dress up in Tudor gowns.

★ Meet characters from Henry VIII's court on a costumed tour.

★ Smell the cooking in the Tudor kitchen.

★ Play hide-and-seek among the yew trees.

★ Spot the animals; there are carvings of lions, dragons and unicorns throughout the palace.

tiring and overwhelming for children. Thankfully there is also a huge garden, so that a tour of the palace can be followed by a romp through the yew trees, a roll down the grassy hills or by getting lost in the glorious yew maze. There are ponds and lakes too, filled with fish and birdlife and a fabulous formal garden with vine and rose arbours. And, in the winter, the lawns in front of the palace are home to a merry-go-round and temporary ice skating rink.

Hampton Court began its life as the home of King Henry VII's courtier Giles Daubeney, who built a modest mansion house on the site. This was turned into a vast and elaborate palace by the next king's chief advisor, Cardinal Thomas Wolsey. Wolsey's Hampton Court reflected his status as the most powerful politician in Britain, with 500 staff and 280 rooms, including lavish private chambers and three suites for his friend Henry VIII, Queen Katherine of Aragon and their daughter Princess Mary. The palace was so magnificent that contemporaneous poet John Skelton famously quipped that "The king's court, Should have the excellence, But Hampton Court Hath the pre-eminence!" When Wolsey failed to obtain a papal annulment, Henry VIII stripped him of his office and his property and took Hampton Court for himself, adding it to his collection of 60 other palaces. Parts of Wolsey's palace still remain, notably **Base Court**, the vast outer courtyard he built to house his guests.

In 10 years Henry spent the Tudor equivalent of £18 million remodelling and extending Hampton Court. He added much of what you see today: a Chapel Royal, tennis courts, bowling alleys, formal gardens, a woodland for hunting, a communal lavatory known as the Great House of Easement (where almost 30 guests could relieve themselves at any one time), a huge kitchen (which is another kids' favourite) and the **Great Hall**, which he used for banquets. A jocular Henry dined here with Jane Seymour on the night he executed Anne Boleyn. Look for the crests of Henry's six wives in the stained-glass windows.

Henry's descendants were more modest, adding little to the building. Shakespeare performed here for James I in the early 1600s. Charles I added ornamental fountains to the gardens and greatly augmented the royal painting collection. Cromwell imprisoned Charles in Hampton Court 15 years later, stripped the palace of its royal fittings,

including gilt work from the Chapel Royal, and sold off many of the monarch's personal possessions. Dutch William III and his Scottish cousin Queen Mary II brought the Glorious Revolution to Hampton Court's Tudor architecture, replacing it with early baroque, remodelled by Christopher Wren and his deputy William Talman. The building's garden façades and much of today's interior decoration date from this period and include sumptuous trompe l'oeil ceiling paintings busy with fat cherubs.

Tudor kitchen at Hampton Court.

William and Mary were also responsible for the yews, the maze and the wonderful herb garden. After their reign, Hampton Court lost royal favour and was last used by George II in 1737.

Hampton Court offers plenty of activities for kids, who can dress up in Tudor outfits, go on costumed tours with characters from the royal courts, listen to a kids' audio guide of the King's Guard Chamber, take one of several family trails or search for ghosts. The palace also has a playroom for under fives located next to the Base Court toilets.

More family favourites

Chiswick House

W5, T020-8742 3905, chgt.org.uk. House Apr daily 1000-1700, May-Oct Sun-Wed 1000-1700, Nov-Mar closed except for group tours. £5, £2.50 child. Gardens daily 0700-dusk. Free. Rail: Chiswick.

There's nowhere more appropriate to appreciate the colours of autumn than in one of the birthplaces of the English landscape garden: Chiswick House. The gardens showcase the work of famous English gardeners including Samuel Lapidge, who was assistant to the most famous Augustan gardener of all, Lancelot 'Capability' Brown. There are extensive lawns, flower beds and acres of stately trees from all over the world, a beautiful Italian walled garden decorated with

Haunted palaces

The Royal Palaces have some famous ghosts. The **Tower of London** (see page 80) is said to be haunted by a giant bear and by the ghosts of Lady Jane Grey and Arabella Stuart, James I's cousin who was imprisoned and probably murdered here. **Buckingham Palace** (see page 46) is said to be haunted by the spirit of Major John Gwynne, an aide to Edward VII who committed suicide there. And the ghost of King George II is said to sit staring from a window in **Kensington Palace** (see page 66). **Hampton Court** has three ghosts. Catherine Howard, Henry's fifth wife is said to haunt the corridor she ran down to plead with Henry for her life, shortly before being executed in 1541. The corridor has such a creepy feel that it is popularly known as the Haunted Gallery. Another figure mysteriously appeared on CCTV footage near to the Clock Court in October 2003, when fire doors were mysteriously blown open with great force and a ghost in period dress appeared to close them. And Dame Sybil Penn, also known as the Grey Lady, who died of smallpox after nursing Elizabeth I through the disease, is said to wander the corridors and courts after dark. A Kids' Ghost Trail around the palace is available on the website or from reception.

Don't miss Royal Botanic Gardens

Kew (Richmond, TW9 3PZ, T020-8332 5655, kew.org, daily 0930-dusk. £13.90, children free, tube: Kew Gardens, rail: Kew Gardens or Key Bridge, boat: Kew Pier) is the world's most famous botanical garden and botanical research institute. The 297-acre gardens and giant Victorian and Edwardian glasshouses preserve the world's largest collection of living plants and the seed of almost every species recorded so far on the planet. The gardens evolved from the private estate of the 17th-century Capel family, who were, perhaps, Britain's first obsessive aristocrat gardeners. The Capel estate was acquired by the monarchy and, in 1759, Princess Augusta and Lord Bute established the first formal botanic gardens on the site. The gardens were expanded greatly by George II.

The institute has changed the course of human history on several occasions: Joseph Banks, Kew's adviser to King George III, chose the site for the Botany Bay colony in Australia in 1788, which would become the city of Sydney; it was a commission for Kew to bring back breadfruit that led to the mutiny on the *Bounty* in 1789; Kew's laboratories first isolated quinine to produce a tonic against malaria in the 19th century, and, in 1876, Henry Wickham of Kew ended the rubber boom in Brazil after rubber seeds smuggled from the Amazon were propagated in Malaysia and India.

The gardens cover so large an area it would be impossible for a fit adult to see everything in a day, so it's important to plan a visit. Here are some highlights for children:

★ The **Princess of Wales Conservatory** was opened by Diana in 1987 with 10 computer-controlled climatic zones grouped under 'dry tropics', with plants from the world's warm, arid areas, and 'wet tropics', with moisture-loving plants from ecosystems like rainforests and mangrove swamps. Look out for the stone plants, the Dracula orchid, the tanks filled with piranha fish and poison dart frogs, the giant water lilies – which can span 6 ft (2 m) across and bear the weight of a baby – and the hundreds of carnivorous plants including big Venus flytraps and sticky sundews. Every year the conservatory hosts a festival celebrating some 1500 species of tropical orchid.

★ The tropical **Palm House** swelters even in the depths of winter and has hundreds of huge palms, cycads and climbers. Don't miss the double coconut palm, which bears the biggest seed in the world and the Marine display, which simulates four marine habitats and their plants.

★ The **Temperate House** is the largest Victorian glass building in the world. Look out for the fruit trees (including lemons and limes and date palms which have more than 800 uses), and plants on the verge

of extinction like the St Helena ebony tree. In 1980 only two specimens were left in the wild, clinging to a steep rock face on the island. Kew botanists took cuttings from these and went on to propagate several thousand plants, which have since been reintroduced at six sites on the island.

★ The **Rhizotron and Xstrata Treetop Walkway** is 59 ft (18 m) above the ground and great for spotting birds and insects.

★ **Climbers and Creepers** is Britain's first interactive botanical play zone, where

three- to nine-year-olds can climb inside a flower to learn about pollination or trap model flies in a giant Venus flytrap.

★ Next to Climbers and Creepers is **Treehouse Towers**, a traditional bark-floored playground with giant swings, zip wires, scramble nets, slides and a mountaineering wall.

There is plenty of information for families on the excellent website, including a Parents' Survival Guide to Kew. The gardens are easy to negotiate with a map, downloadable from the website or available at any of the entrances.

66 99
Kew Gardens has really cool games to play. It makes me feel cheerful because there are plants and flowers to smell and galleries to see. It is a fantastic place to start the day.

Sofia, aged 10

classical statues and a camellia hothouse with the finest flowers in London outside Kew. The gardens surround Chiswick House, one of the finest surviving examples of Palladian architecture in the country, and containing superb collections of Renaissance paintings and classical English and European furniture. There are also tennis courts which are free to use, if the weather is up to it.

Ham House

Ham St, TW10 7RS, T020-8940 1950, nationaltrust.org.uk. House Feb-Mar daily 1130-1530 (for tours of selected room only), Apr-Oct daily 1200-1600, Nov daily 1130-1500, Dec-Jan closed. Gardens Nov-Feb daily 1100-1600, Mar-Oct daily 1100-1700. Prices vary throughout the year, up to £10 (£3.65 garden only), up to £6.05 child (£1.10 garden only). Rail and tube: Richmond and bus 371.

This red-brick Stuart mansion is one of the grandest houses along the banks of the Thames with beautiful 17th-century interiors, historically important gardens and an outstanding collection of furniture and textiles. The house's most famous owner was Elizabeth Countess of Dysart, outwardly a friend of Oliver Cromwell (who regularly dined at Ham House) but, in reality, a member of the Sealed Knot, a secret Royalist organization. Elizabeth travelled between Ham and France to carry coded letters from supporters to the exiled Charles Stuart. After he was restored to the throne, Charles II rewarded the countess with an annual pension of £800; she lived an extravagant life at Ham with her second husband John Maitland, second Earl of Lauderdale.

Not that the furniture or colourful history will draw many

children; they will want to visit because Ham House is said to be one of the most haunted in Britain. Ghosts have been reported here since the 19th century, when, according to writer Augustus Hare, a butler's daughter is said to have seen a little old woman scratching the wall close to the fireplace. The old woman stared at the child and "So horrible was her stare, that the child was terrified and screamed and hid her face." Since then footprints have been seen in the bedchamber of the countess, her cane has been heard tapping on the floorboards and in the chapel, and caretakers have seen the ghost of a dog haunting the grounds. All of these ghostly sightings are gloriously exploited on the after-dark Hallowe'en ghost tours (see the website for details).

Hogarth's House

Hogarth Lane, Great West Rd, W4 2QN, hounslow.info. Mon-Fri 1300-1600, Sat-Sun 1300-1700. Free. Tube: Turnham Green, rail: Chiswick.
For a glimpse of daily London life in the 18th century, head for the former home of the period's most famous cartoonist and engraver, William Hogarth. The house is packed with his paintings, drawings and memorabilia, which caricature and satirize the life of the city. Look out for Hogarth's most famous engraving, *The Rake's Progress*, depicting the descent

Ham House.

into debauchery of a young man who comes into money.

Kew Bridge Steam Museum

Green Dragon Lane, Brentford, TW8 0EN, T020-8568 4757, kbsm.org. Tue-Sun 1100-1600. £9.50, £3.50 child (valid for a year). Rail: Kew Bridge. For a century, London's water supply was pumped by the five gargantuan steam engines on display in this odd little museum situated in a 19th-century pumping station. These are preserved alongside the city's only steam railway, powered by tiny steam engines, which kids get to ride (Apr-Oct Sun only). The body of the museum tells the story of the city's water supply. This is less turgid than it sounds, with plenty of hands-on activities, including crawling through sewer tunnels, sieving for lost coins as slum-dwelling kids did in Victorian times and searching for wildlife with a remote-controlled sewer robot.

Musical Museum

399 High St, Brentford, TW8 0DU, T020-8560 8108, musicalmuseum. co.uk. Tue-Sun 1100-1730, guided tours Tue, Sat-Sun 1430, Fri 1130. £8, under 16s free. Rail: Kew Bridge or Brentford.

This tiny museum is home to one of the world's largest collections of mechanical, self-playing instruments. These include all manner of musical boxes, self-playing pianos, organs and violins as well as

'orchestrions' and 'orchestrelles', which were both designed to simulate an orchestra. Look out for the 'Mighty Wurlitzer': a 'one man orchestra' installed in movie theatres in the USA to accompany silent films. This rises up through the floor during some of the museum's film showings and concerts (see website for schedule). Visit the museum on a guided tour to see all the instruments in action.

Osterley House & Park

Jersey Rd, Isleworth, TW7 4RB, T020-8232 5050, nationaltrust.org.uk. House Mar-Oct Wed-Sun 1200-1630, Dec Sat-Sun 1230-1530. £9.20, £4.60 child. Gardens Mar-Oct Wed-Sun 1000-1700, £4. Tube: Osterley and bus H28.

A large lawned park surrounds this stately home by Robert Adam. It has Adam's trademark lavish, colourful interiors as well as Tudor stables and a 'below stairs' area with exhibits on what life was like as a servant.

Syon House & Park

Syon Park, TW8 8JF, syonpark.co.uk. Mid-Mar to Oct Wed-Thu, Sun and bank hols 1100-1700, closed Nov to mid-Mar. House and park £10, £4 child, £22 family. Gardens only £5, £2.50 child, £11 family. Rail: Syon Lane or Brentford.

Syon House is the last surviving duke's residence complete with its country estate in Greater London. It is a superb late Tudor stately home, with baroque and neoclassical additions, and has been the London home of the Duke of Northumberland for more than 400 years. The building has a colourful history with gory details which will interest kids more than the opulent painted interiors. It was originally a Bridgettine Abbey – named after Mount Zion in Israel – but was dissolved by Henry VIII. The king stripped the abbey of its treasures, executed the Father Confessor and had his body chained to the abbey gateposts. He then gave the abbey to the Duke of Somerset, Edward Seymour, brother of the king's third wife Jane and Lord Protector of his young son, Edward (later Edward VI). Somerset demolished it and built the current house as a private home. But, it seems, the abbey had its revenge. In 1547 when the king's coffin was being transported to Windsor for burial, the funeral troupe stayed at Syon House. Henry's coffin burst open during the night and guards found his corpse half-eaten by dogs in the morning.

After Henry's death, Somerset effectively ruled on behalf of the boy King Edward VI. He was deposed in 1550 and executed at the Tower of London two years later and Syon House passed to the Duke of Northumberland, the new de facto ruler of the country. The 15-year-old king fell seriously ill in February 1553 and pledged his crown to the

great-granddaughter of Henry VII, Lady Jane Grey, who by happy coincidence or political sleight of hand was married to the Duke of Northumberland's son, Lord Guildford Dudley. On Edward's death, Jane was presented with the crown at Syon House before being transported to London by boat and proclaimed Queen. Her reign lasted for nine days before she was summarily removed by Henry VIII's eldest daughter, Mary Tudor, and executed, together with Dudley and his children, in the Tower of London (see page 80).

In the 18th century, the Tudor house was completely redesigned by Robert Adam, who is responsible for the lavish, colourful interiors you see today. Capability Brown designed the gardens.

There is plenty to entertain kids at Syon. The beautiful gardens filled with rare trees and dotted with lakes and ponds are great for a run-around. There's a huge early Victorian glasshouse filled with subtropical plants, an indoor adventure playground, **Snakes & Ladders** (T020-8847 0946, snakes-and-ladders.co.uk, daily 1000-1800, £1, £7.30 over 5s, £6.30 under 5s, £5.30 under 2s, not included in the Syon House ticket) and a small zoo, **Tropical Forest** (T020-8847 4730, tropicalforest.co.uk, daily 1000-1730, closed 25-26 Dec and 1 Jan, £6.50 , £5.50 child, £22 family, not included in Syon

House ticket), which recreates a series of rainforest environments and has animals including Brazilian marmosets (monkeys as small as a kitten), poison dart frogs, boas and baby crocodiles.

Wimbledon Windmill Museum

Windmill Rd, Wimbledon Common, SW19 5NR, T020-8947 2825, wimbledonwindmill.org.uk. Apr-Oct Sat 1400-1700, Sun 1100-1700. £2, £1 child, £5 family. Tube and rail: Wimbledon.
Richmond spreads north to merge with **Wimbledon Common**, made famous by the foraging Wombles. It has nine lakes, babbling brooks and one of the few remaining windmills in London. This houses modest displays and audio-visual exhibits describing the history of the mill and how windmills in general work, as well as hands on exhibits where kids can grind wheat into flour and chaff and climb a ladder to the gallery for London views.

Action stations

Cycling

The best way to explore Richmond Park is on a bike. Cycle paths run the perimeter and cut through the centre of the park and are marked on free cycle maps (Nos 9 and 10 on tfl.gov. uk). Mountain and road bikes and various bike add-ons for children can be hired through **Parkcycle** at the Roehampton Gate car park and café area in Richmond Park (£7/hr off peak and £9 peak); arrive early in summer to ensure you get one.

Skate boarding
Bay 66 (55-66 Acklam Rd, W10 5YU, T020-8969 4699, baysixty6. com, Mon-Fri 1100-2100, Sat-Sun 1000-2100, £3 beginners, £6 all others, tube: Westbourne Park or Ladbroke Grove) is one of the best-equipped skateboard parks in London with ramps, bowls and plenty of open space.

Anyone for tennis?

The world's greatest lawn tennis tournament takes place at the All England Lawn Tennis and Croquet Club in Wimbledon Park in June, with the finals usually played on the first weekend of July. Around 500 tickets for the show courts (Centre Court, Court No 1 and Court No 2) are held at the turnstiles each day (except for the last four days); expect to queue overnight for a chance to buy one. Easier to come by are the 6000 ground admission tickets, which are available each day for entry to the Court No 2 standing enclosure and for unreserved seating and standing on the outside courts. Once ground capacity has been reached, queuers are admitted on a one-out, one-in basis. It is also possible to visit Wimbledon for around £12 after 1700 on weekdays to watch games on the outer courts, soak up the atmosphere and throng around the big screen on 'Henman Hill'. The club also runs the **Wimbledon Lawn Tennis Museum** (wimbledon.org, daily 1000-1700 – ticket holders only during the championships – closed middle Sun of championships, Mon after championships, 24-26 Dec, 1 Jan, £11, £6 child, under 5s free), which tells the story of the competition with displays of tennis-related gear, state-of-the-art audio-visual displays and trophies.

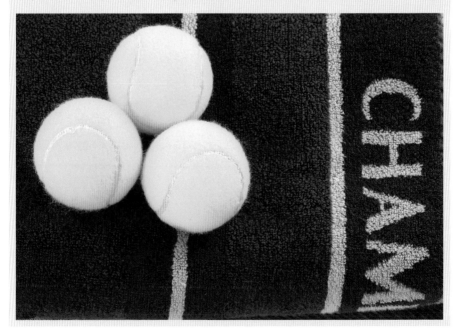

Contents

East End street art.

East London

You must

❶ Have a foot in both hemispheres on the Meridian line in Greenwich.

❷ Dress up in 18th-century costumes at the Greenwich Discovery Centre.

❸ Play guitar along to your favourite song at the British Music Experience.

❹ Smell the stench of medieval London at the Museum of London Docklands.

❺ Float among the stars in the Royal Observatory.

❻ March through the marshes in Hackney and Wanstead.

❼ Be a Victorian kid for the day at the Ragged School Museum.

❽ Take a candlelit tour at Dennis Severs' House.

❾ See some Brit Art in hip Hoston.

❿ Watch a show in the Millennium Dome.

East London stretches north and south of the river beyond the City of London, and includes the East End, the Docklands and the new Royal Borough of Greenwich.

In a century the **East End** has changed from the sordid slums of Conan Doyle's days, to half-abandoned urban wasteland in the post-war years and, in the last decade, into one of London's most fashionable regions. Its throbbing clubs and boho bars will hold little interest for kids, but they'll love its funky graffiti-daubed streets and might enjoy the bizarre Brit Art in its galleries. The **Docklands** glisten with new developments, including the spires of Canary Wharf, that are a delight to wander around with kids, especially when visited in conjunction with the new **Museum of London Docklands**, which tells the story of the port of London from its heyday to today. **Greenwich** is a destination its own right, bursting with heritage, with a string of world-class museums, some fabulous buildings and plenty of greenery to rush about in. A little further east are two iconic engineering marvels: the **Millennium Dome** and the **Thames Barrier**, whose sturdy gates keep London from flooding.

A day out at Greenwich.

Out & about East London

See some Brit Art

Hoxton Square, Brick Lane and northern Whitechapel are some of the most modish districts in contemporary London, with the coolest alternative nightlife, funky shops and a number of fashionable galleries, all of which have interesting, usually free exhibitions of controversial modern art. **White Cube** (48 Hoxton Sq, N1 6PB, T020-7930 5373, whitecube.com, Tue-Sat 1000-1800, tube: Old Street) is run by art empresario Jay Jopling and principally showcases the work of the so-called New British Artists (NBAs). But you can also see megastars of the now increasingly old

Street art

There is simply nowhere better in Britain to see cutting-edge graffiti than the East End of London, especially along **Brick Lane** (see above and pages 16 and 181), the **Regent's Canal** (see page 89) and around **Rivington Street** in Hoxton. Banksy, the world's most famous graffiti artist since Basquiat, has long used east London as one of his favourite canvases and has inspired dozens of other graffiti artists to do the same. Although it was once outlawed, much of the graffiti is either encouraged or commissioned as street art by local authorities, shops and businesses.

guard, including Damien Hirst (famous for his sharks and sheep in aspic), Turner-prize nominee, Tracey Emin, and satiricial conceptual artists, Jake and Dinos Chapman. (Some parents might consider some of the exhibitions unsuitable for children.) **Rivington Place** (EC2A 3BA, T020-7749 1240, rivingtonplace.org, Tue, Wed, Fri 1100-1800, Thu 1100-2100, Sat 1200-1800, tube: Old Street, Liverpool Street or Shoreditch High Street) shows visual arts and installations, and the longer-established **Whitechapel Gallery** (77-82 Whitechapel High St, E1 7QX, T020-7522 7888, whitechapelgallery.org, Tue-Wed and Fri-Sun 1100-1800, Thu 1100-2100, tube: Aldgate East and Liverpool Street) hosts the best of the older crowd of post-modernists, including Jackson Pollock and David Hockney.

March through the marshes
The **Hackney and Walthamstow Marshes** (leevalleypark.org.uk, tube: Blackhorse Road or Tottenham Hale, rail: Hackney Wick or Clapton) are a vast green area extending north from Hackney towards the Epping Forest (see page 94). The marshes are a remnant of London's once widespread wetlands and river valley grasslands; the reaches next to the River Lea and Hackney Cut are home to rare birds and wild flowers. This is a great area for a walk or a cycle ride; the marshes and fields are crossed by numerous paths, the prettiest of which runs parallel to the River Lea, which is always busy with colourful wooden barges and visited by herons, swans, kingfishers and numerous ducks and rails. Look out for the herd of old longhorn cows which wander the marshes keeping the grass trim.

Park life: East London

In addition to **Greenwich Park** (see page 140), east London has some great, often little-visited parks. **London Fields** (E8, hackney.gov.uk, rail: London Fields) is a small green space in Hackney with London's only heated lido (T020-7254 9038, hackney.gov.uk, opening times vary, £4.10, £2.45 child). The park has a decent playground and a paddling pool (end May-Sep Tue-Wed and Fri-Sun 1100-1900). The London Fields pub (thelondonfields.com) overlooking the park serves food and has outdoor tables for kids. Nearby, **Victoria Park** (E9, towerhamlets.gov.uk, rail: Cambridge Heath or Hackney Wick) is perhaps the most attractive park in east London. It sits next to the Regent's Canal and covers some

87 acres, with extensive lawns, lovely formal gardens, avenues of trees and a large lake. In summer the park hosts open-air music festivals. The park has excellent facilities for kids: a playground with a summer paddling pool, a club for under fives, and herds of deer and goats. On the first Sunday in July the Victoria Model Steam Boat Club, founded in the park on 15 July 1904, holds the largest of its 20 annual regattas. **Thames Barrier Park** (E16, lda.gov.uk, DLR: Pontoon Dock), a pretty, award-winning green space on the north bank of the river, is a good place to see the Thames Barrier. The unusual gardens, which are great for a game of hide-and-seek, comprise a series of undulating hedges, interrupted by long lawns

and overlooked by boardwalks. They were designed by French landscape architect Alain Provost, famous for the Parc Floral in the Bois de Vincennes, Paris.

London's top five parks for winter sledging

Alexandra Park (see page 102).

Brockwell Park (see page 111).

Greenwich Park (see page 140).

Hampstead Heath – Parliament Hill (see page 92).

Primrose Hill (see page 89).

" My favourite thing to do in London is to go to Victoria Park because it makes you feel happy and makes you smile. You can explore the park, ride your bike and the best thing is to eat ice cream and play on the equipment.

Simony, aged eight

Don't miss Greenwich

Greenwich has gone from tawdry to top tourist attraction in the last 20 years. The borough became Britain's 17th UNESCO World Heritage Site in 1997 and, to mark the Queen's Diamond Jubilee in 2012, will join Kensington and Chelsea, Windsor and Kingston as London's fourth Royal Borough. There's more than enough here for a full family day. Begin a trip first thing in the morning on the good-value and exhilarating **Thames Clipper** (see page 22), which leaves from a string of piers in central London. (Alternative transport is DLR: Cutty Sark or rail: Greenwich.) Then, pick and mix a sightseeing day from Greenwich's assortment of attractions.

The boat stops at Greenwich pier right in front of the **Cutty Sark** (2 Greenwich Church St, SE10, T020-8858 2698, cuttysark.org.uk), the world's only surviving 19th-century commercial wooden sailing ship. This incredible ship has been beloved of children since she opened as a museum in the 1950s, and her towering masts, beautiful lines and countless romantic sea-faring stories still stimulate the imagination today. The *Cutty Sark* was built in 1869 and used in the tea and wool trades, which had developed from mere merchant transport to become an intensely competitive race across the world between Australia, the Far East and London. The *Cutty Sark* was built expressly

My favourite thing in London is the Thames Clipper boat ride to Greenwich. I love it because you can really feel the spirit of the sea and it makes me feel happy. You can catch it from right next to the London Eye.

Raphael, aged seven

for the purpose of beating the fastest boat on the water at the time, the *Thermopylae*. In 1885 she set the record passage of 73 days from Sydney to London and, on one occasion, even overhauled the fastest steam ship on the route, the *Britannia*. The *Cutty Sark* was badly damaged in a fire in 2007 but, as this book went to press, was expected to reopen to the public mid-2012; check the website.

A hundred metres or so in front of the *Cutty Sark*, in a splendid neoclassical building overlooked by a statue of Walter Raleigh, is the newly opened **Discover Greenwich Visitor Centre** (Old Royal Naval College 2, Cutty Sark Gardens, SE10, T020-8269 4747, oldroyalnavalcollege. org, daily 1000-1700, free), a mix of museum, temporary exhibition centre and tourist office. There's plenty for kids here. They can dress up in 18th-century costumes, construct their own buildings, explore dozens of interactive screens telling the story of royal and maritime Greenwich and sit on a berth in a tiny 18th-century

Don't miss Greenwich

facsimile sailor's quarters. There's a microbrewery in the building for thirsty adults and a large tourist office with helpful staff and maps and leaflets on all the borough's attractions. The centre is the gateway to Christopher Wren's magnificent **Old Royal Naval College**, now home to Greenwich University and Trinity College of Music (listen out for pianos tinkling and brass blowing in the practice rooms). Only the Painted Hall (with a magnificent trompe l'oeil ceiling) and the chapel are open to the public.

Across the road is the imposing **National Maritime Museum** (Romney Rd, SE10 9NF, T020-8858 4422, nmm.ac.uk, daily 1000-1700, free), which tells the story of Britain's seafaring between the 16th and early 20th centuries. It's a large museum with many galleries but be sure to see the Explorers gallery, telling the story of Europe's great discoveries, the Trafalgar exhibition, which has Nelson's uniform, complete with fatal musket hole, and the ornate 62-ft (19-m) long barge, built for Frederick, Prince of Wales, eldest son of George II. The All Hands and Bridge galleries are designed for children, who can send a semaphore signal, load a cargo ship, man the bridge as captain, read maritime charts and attempt to plot a course, and even fire a cannon.

The museum also administers the 17th-century Queen's House and the Royal Observatory and Planetarium. The **Queen's House** (details as for National Maritime Museum), just west of the museum, was the first Palladian building in England designed by Inigo Jones and is stuffed full of paintings, most of which (other than the naval battle scenes) will leave kids cold. But they'll enjoy the Great Hall with its striking black-and-white floors and the spiralling Tulip stairs.

From the Maritime Museum, spend some time in **Greenwich Park** (royalparks.gov.uk), which covers 183 acres of woodland and lawns. It's a wonderful spot for a run-around and for sledging in winter. There are small herds of fallow and red deer and fabulous river views. Climb through the park to the **Royal Observatory** (details as for National Maritime Museum), which sits high on the hill, plumb on the Greenwich Meridian line; you can stand either side of the line with one foot in the eastern and the other foot in the western hemisphere. Look out for the red Time Ball on top of the dome, which lowers at precisely 1300 daily. Inside the observatory is one of the largest optical telescopes in the world and a museum telling the story of latitude, longitude and the demarcation of time. Next door is a superb **planetarium**, which runs around 10 shows a day, suitable for kids of all ages, who will be amazed as they whizz through the gas clouds of Jupiter or the rings of Saturn.

Out & about East London

Brunel Museum

Railway Av, SE16 4LF, T020-7231 3840, brunel-museum.org.uk. Daily 1000-1700. £2, £1 concessions, under 16s free. Tube: Rotherhithe.

This museum is devoted to the engineering exploits of father and son Marc and Isambard Kingdom Brunel but the main draw for visiting kids are the spooky tunnel tours. These follow parts of the old pedestrian Thames Tunnel, built in 1843 as the first tunnel beneath a major navigable river. The engineering project was deemed such a marvel that the press called it the Eighth Wonder of the World. On the first day of opening 50,000 people walked through; within the first 10 weeks 1,000,000 people from all over Europe visited the tunnel (half the population of the capital at the time). Those Victorian visitors were entertained by street performers and touted by vendors, an experience roughly reproduced today in the museum. The rest of the museum, whose galleries sit in the old Victorian engine house, tells the story of the tunnel's construction.

Dennis Severs' House

8 Folgate St, E1 6BX, T020-7247 4013, dennissevershouse.co.uk. Sun 1200-1600. £8; 1st and 3rd Mon of month 1200-1400, £5. Silent Night tour Mon 1800-2100, £12 adult and child (book in advance). Tube: Liverpool Street.

If possible, visit this minutely and exactly reproduced 18th-century Huguenot silk-weaver's house on the Monday 'Silent Night' candlelit tour (although it's only suitable for children who can be quiet for 45 minutes!). It's as if you have somehow stumbled through a time tunnel into someone's private home. Bottles lie strewn on a table in one room, food is half-eaten on a plate in another, a ruffled silk counterpane lies on an unmade four-poster bed in another. The smell of food fills the air throughout, and you can hear the muffled voices of conversations that seem to be conducted just around the corner of every door or window. Each room holds a historical clue which older kids can unravel to discover something about the East End and about a fictional event which unfolded in the house. In the cellar, for instance, there's a crater with fragments of St Mary's Spital, the church that gave its name to nearby Spitalfields. The house was created by Californian designer, Dennis Severs, who lived here until 1999.

Eltham Palace

Eltham, SE9 5QE, english-heritage. org.uk. Nov, Dec, Feb and Mar Sun-Wed 1100-1600 (closed 24-26 Dec and all Jan); for summer opening, see the website. £8.70, £7.40 concessions, £4.40 child. Rail: Eltham or Mottingham, then bus.

Eltham Palace is an architectural pantomime horse. It's one of the few substantially intact medieval royal palaces in Britain, with a sweeping grand hall and moat, but it's also an art deco fantasy mansion built by millionaire textile industrialist and art collector, Stephen Courtauld, and added onto the original hall in the 1930s. Both portions of the building are preserved as in aspic. Children will love the ocean-liner glamour of the Courtauld home, which looks like a set from a movie. They'll enjoy rushing about the gardens too, whose nooks and crannies are filled with gorgeous plants. There are lawns, a sunken rose garden, a spring bulb meadow, a rock garden, woodland, a Tudor bridge and (dry) moat and wonderful crumbling medieval ruins. Little ponds fill with tadpoles and newts in summer. The palace has planned activity trails around the house and gardens for kids to follow and stages various events in the summer months, which are advertised on the website. Pushchairs are not permitted in the building.

Eltham Palace.

This small museum is worth visiting in conjunction with the Museum of Childhood in Bethnal Green (see below). The permanent display tells the stories of some of the multitude of people from all over the world who have made their homes in Hackney since Saxon times. You can hear interviews on handsets situated throughout the display, retelling recent immigrants' experiences. Engaging hands-on activities include loading a Saxon boat, dressing up in historical costume and Victorian matchbox making. Touch screens enable visitors to view online exhibitions, map family histories or take a virtual tour of a Victorian household.

Geffrye Museum

136 Kingsland Rd, E2 8EA, T020-7739 9893, geffrye-museum.org.uk. Tue-Sat 1000-1700, Sun and bank hols 1200-1700, closed 1 Jan, Good Fri, 24-26 Dec. £2, free child. Tube: Old Street, rail: Hoxton.

Each of the 11 rooms in these elegant former almshouses offers a glimpse of middle-class London life through the centuries. They come complete with original furniture, paintings and period pieces, beginning with the 17th century and running up to the present. Part of the museum is

The Geffrye Museum is so interesting and it makes me feel curious.

Maisie, aged eight

devoted to a completely restored 18th-century almshouse (open to visitors on selected days only), which reproduces the living conditions of London's poor and elderly in the 1780s and 1880s. There are activity sheets for kids, who can use them to solve puzzles and follow trails around the museum. A good value al fresco restaurant, overlooking the pretty herb gardens, serves contemporary and traditional English food, soups, sandwiches and salads.

Hackney Museum

1 Reading Lane, E8 1GQ, T020-8356 3500, hackney.gov.uk. Tue-Wed and Fri 0930-1730, Thu 0930-2000, Sat 1000-1700. Gardens Apr-Oct Tue-Sat 1000-1700, Sun 1200-1700. Free. Rail: Hackney Central.

Museum of Childhood

Cambridge Heath Rd, Bethnal Green, E2 9PA, T020-8983 5200, vam.ac.uk. Daily 1000-1745 (until 2100 on the first Thu of the month). Free. Tube: Bethnal Green.

This east London wing of the V&A (see page 64) houses a huge collection of items relating to childhood, from toys and games to clothing, furniture, prams, babies' bottles, christening gifts and even nappies. The collections offer a fascinating insight into children's lives over the centuries but as all the tantalizing toys and games are kept well beyond the reach of small hands, it can feel a little dry for children.

The Millennium Dome, now called the O2 Centre.

> I like going to the O2 Centre to watch a basketball match, because it looks soooo cool when someone reaches up and touches the basketball net and scores.

Anna, aged seven

Museum of London Docklands

West India Quay, Canary Wharf, E14 4AL, museumindocklands.org.uk. Daily 1000-1800, closed 24-26 Dec. Free. Tube: DLR West India Quay or Canary Wharf, boat: Canary Wharf pier.

The eastern outpost of the Museum of London (see page 78) is housed in a large Victorian sugar warehouse right in the heart of the docklands, within easy reach of the sky-scrapers and the Docklands Light Railway. It tells the story of the port of London from the earliest settlement to its zenith as the world's biggest and busiest in the 19th and early 20th centuries. After a thorough refurbishment, the museum now mixes traditional exhibitions with some of the most imaginative hands-on and digital displays in the capital. Children will be moved and appalled by the London, Sugar and Slavery gallery on floor three, which combines video footage, panels, artefacts, and sound and visual effects to tell the story of the transatlantic slave trade. The Sailortown model village assaults all the senses, with the sounds, sights and smells of the old port city, while the Jack the Ripper exhibit tells the story not only of the famous Whitechapel murders but the squalid day-to-day life of contemporaneous east Londoners. Staff are very helpful and really look after young visitors: pushchairs are welcome throughout, there's free mineral water and even fold-up chairs you can carry around with you to sit on when it all gets too much. The museum has a decent café-restaurant and there are plenty of other eating options on the doorstep.

O2 Centre & the British Music Experience

SE10 0DX, T020-8463 2000, theo2. co.uk. For details of events and bookings, see the website.

The Millennium Dome now rechristened the O2, since reopening as the city's premier concert venue in 2007, is one of east London's most impressive and iconic architectural sights, impressive for kids and adults alike. It is the largest steel and tensioned fabric tent in the world, with a shell 365 m in diameter (1 m for each day of the year) supported by a dozen 100-m high steel columns (one for each month). The concert space is the best large arena in the capital and has hosted big acts like Led Zeppelin, the Black Eyed Peas, Bon Jovi, Rihanna and Madonna, along with sporting events and spectaculars. The 2012 Olympic gymnastics events will be performed here. The O2 also has a smaller venue (the indigO2), the O2 bubble exhibition centre, a nightclub, dozens of chain restaurants, an 11-screen cinema (myvue. com), shops and a brand new culture museum, the **British Music Experience** (britishmusicexperience.com, daily 1100-1930, closed 24-26 Dec and 31 Dec-2 Jan, £10, £6 child, under 5s free). The museum charts the course of British popular music from 1945 to the present day. Although the space is small, it manages to pack in a chronology of the music from trad jazz and skiffle through early rock and the heyday of the late sixties and seventies to TV talent shows, Simon Cowell and the present day. There's loads of memorabilia for grown-ups, with costumes and instruments behind the glass and a huge archive of vintage audio and

video to listen to, much of it from shows like *Top of the Pops* or *The Tube*. Children, however, who have no memory of these will prefer the Gibson Studio, where they can try their hand at keyboards, drums or electric guitars. After a five-minute class, they are handed the instruments and told to play along with a chosen track. By swiping the entrance ticket, they can save their performance for home. They will also enjoy the Dance the Decades booth, where they can groove along to 60 years of dance music: rocking and rolling with Cliff, bopping to the Beatles, boogying to Hot Chocolate or getting jiggy with Jessie J; all dances can be filmed for your future amusement.

Ragged School Museum

46-50 Copperfield Rd, E3 4RR, T020-8980 6405, raggedschoolmuseum. org.uk. Wed-Thu 1000-1700, 1st Sun of month 1400-1700. Free for galleries, charges for classroom sessions. Tube: Mile End, DLR Limehouse.

Kids get the chance to discover that they've never had it so good with a taste of classroom life in this simulated Victorian Dr Barnardo's Ragged School next to pretty Regent's Canal. The classes are as close as possible to the real thing, with children dressing up in (very clean and well laundered) period clothes, taking notes on hand-held blackboards and being placed in the dunce's hat for minor infractions. Starchy

school ma'ams dish out short shrift and the three Rs but without raps on the knuckles or canings. The museum also exhibits all manner of small items relating to Victorian school and home life, from dip pens, ink bottles, ink wells and ink pourers to tin mugs, plates, carpet beaters, pegs and Victorian sewing machines.

Royal Artillery Museum

Royal Arsenal, Woolwich, SE18 6ST, T020-8855 7755, firepower.org.uk. £5.30, £2.50 child, £12.50 family £12.50. Rail: Woolwich Arsenal.

This is London's most gung-ho war museum. Tanks, giant howitzers, anti-aircraft guns, missile launchers and a wealth of horse-drawn guns from the 18th and 19th centuries mean that it will appeal principally to boys of all ages. Further displays tell the story of guns since their invention over 700 years ago, and there are galleries of uniforms, drawings, displays of diaries and medals and a 'ground shaking' *Field of Fire* film, in which kids can experience the sound and fury of an artillery battle with shells whizzing overhead and guns booming. The collection is housed in the Royal Arsenal, one of the largest centres in the world for arms manufacture until the late 20th century.

Thames Barrier

1 Unity Way, SE18 5NJ, T020-8305 4188, environment-agency.gov.uk. Apr-Sep daily 1030-1630, Oct-Mar daily 1100-1530. £3.50, £2 child, under 5s free. Rail: Charlton. Spanning 520 m across the River Thames at Woolwich, the Thames Barrier is one of the largest movable flood barriers in the world. It has protected 78 sq miles of central London from flooding caused by tidal surges since 1982. Ten steel gates, each of which weighs over 3000 tons, can be raised across the river at the highest tides, standing as high as a five-storey building and as wide as the opening of Tower Bridge. The best views of the barrier are from the visitor centre on the south bank and from the Thames Barrier Park (see page 137).

Action stations

Activity days & workshops

The **National Maritime Museum** (nmm.ac.uk, see page 140) has plenty of activities for children, both seasonally and weekly. There are special play days for under fives every Tuesday. On Saturdays children of six and over can meet a historical character and participate in a performance bringing maritime history to life, and on Sundays staff conduct historical discover days. The **Museum of Childhood** (vam.ac.uk, see page 143) runs an extensive programme of daily and seasonal activities, which include arts and crafts, storytelling, drama and cooking. Check the 'What's On' pages of the website for details. A wealth of imaginative family activities are on offer at the **Museum of London Docklands** (museumindocklands.org.uk, see page 144). These involve a mix of creative activities, performance and re-enactment, storytelling and exploratory trails around the museum. There are 'messy' and 'musical' activities for under fives and drop-in events at weekends, plus a range of seasonal events for all ages.

Riding

Mudchute Farm (see page 91) has a British Horse Society-approved riding school with 25 horses and ponies, offering lessons to adults and children aged seven and over.

Thames Barrier.

Contents

Dressing up on Brighton beach.

Around London

TERRY

You must

❶ Go crabbing in rockpools in Brighton.

❷ Run around the ramparts at Bodiam or Dover castle.

❸ Hear lions roar outside the car window at Whipsnade.

❹ Take a white-knuckle ride at Thorpe Park.

❺ Ride on steam trains and traction engines at the Hollycombe Steam Collection.

❻ Spot birds and butterflies on the Downs.

❼ Splash in the waves at Cuckmere Haven.

❽ Explore Roman ruins throughout the South.

❾ Take a big day out in Legoland.

❿ Dress up as a knight at the Herstmonceux Medieval Fayre.

Families with more time on their hands might want to explore some of the attractions that lie within easy reach of the city. There's a great deal to see less than an hour's train ride away.

A dozen of Britain's most majestic castles lie on the fringes of London, including **Dover**, perched on top of the famous white cliffs, and **Bodiam**, whose ramparts and moat look like they belong in a story book. There are sandy beaches at **Southend** (all of them with Blue Flag awards for cleanliness) and more bright lights on the pier at London's favourite seaside resort, **Brighton**. There are theme parks like **Thorpe Park**, with its white-knuckle rides, and **Legoland** (which is as great for tots as it is for teens), and wildlife parks like **Whipsnade**, where you can drive across grassy plains grazed by zebras and rhinos. **St Albans**, Dover and a string of other towns preserve some of the most complete Roman ruins in Britain. Others, like **Canterbury** and **Chichester**, are home to some of the finest cathedrals in Europe. There are even wild spots: the winding river and marshlands of **Cuckmere Haven**, which sit below towering cliffs, the chalk **North** and **South Downs**, which are coloured by brightly blooming wild flowers and busy butterflies in spring, and the bird-filled wetlands of **Romney Marsh**. With so much to see, we can offer little more than a few suggestions here.

All the fun of the fair.

Fun & free

Spot butterflies

The **North Downs** are a ridge of chalk hills that separate south London from the southern home counties before stretching southeast through the Medway Valley to meet the South Downs at Dover. They are fringed by meadows and fields and covered for much of their length with thick woodlands, which overflow with bird and mammal life. There are two designated Areas of Outstanding Natural Beauty: the **Surrey Hills** (surreyhills. org), easily accessible from London, and the **Kent Downs** (kentdowns.org.uk), which cover nearly a quarter of the county of Kent from the Medway towns to the white cliffs of Dover. Both offer countless walks, wildlife sights, pretty villages and monuments. Most can be visited from the **North Downs Way** (northdownsway.co.uk), a national trail that runs 156 miles through the hills between Guildford and Dover.

The **Surrey Hills** (which can be accessed from numerous railway stations on the fringes of London) are home to a wealth of rare plants and animals, most notably butterflies. The best places to spot them include **Box Hill** (Tadworth, KT20 7LB, T01306-885502, nationaltrust. org.uk, rail: Boxhill), a 954-acre site owned by the National Trust

that is covered with some of the oldest and most important box tree and yew woodland in Britain. Over two-thirds of British butterfly species have been recorded here. Also try **Ranmore Common**, **Denbies Hillside** and **White Downs** (rail: Dorking), areas of ancient woodland filled with rare British plants like man orchid, columbine and nettle-leafed bellflower, which attract purple hairstreak, Adonis blue and white admiral. Another good spot is the **Devil's Punch Bowl** (near Hindhead, T01428-608771, nationaltrust.org.uk), a large stretch of downland heath with wonderful Wealden views.

Fly a kite

The **South Downs** are a fringe of high chalk hills, covered with meadows and patchy

woodlands, that stretch across much of southern East Sussex. Like the North Downs they are cut by an ancient footpath, the **South Downs Way** (southdownsway.co.uk), which can be accessed from towns and cities along the way. Don't miss the views out over Sussex from the Iron Age hill fort at **Ditchling Beacon** (West Meaton, BN6, sussexwt. org.uk), flying a kite at **Devil's Dyke** (near Saddlescombe, BN45, nationaltrust.org.uk), which can be reached on the No 77 bus from Brighton (two children travel free with a paying adult), or the breathtaking cliff-top views from the **Seven Sisters** (sevensisters.org.uk) and infamous **Beachy Head** (beachyhead.org.uk).

Chessington World of Adventures

Leatherhead Rd, KT9 2NE, T0870-444 7777, chessington.com. Late Mar-Oct daily 1000-1700, extended hours during school hols, closed Dec-mid Mar except for Zoo Days. £12, £7.80 under 12s, children under 1 m free, £24-37 family. Rail: Chessington South. Chessington is one of the better-value theme parks in easy reach of London, with a one-off payment for almost all the rides and attractions. It also caters well for all ages. Highlights include the Land of Dragons (with a puppet theatre for the younger kids and soft play areas for toddlers), the Sea Life Centre (with lots of touch tanks and an Indian ocean tank with black-tip reef sharks), the Wanyama village (a Surrey take on an African rural community with Grevy's zebra and scimitar-horned oryx) and the Trail of Kings, where there are western lowland gorillas, Asiatic lions, Persian leopards, Sumatran tigers, Asian bear cats (binturongs) and Madagascan fossas. Hard-core rides include the vertiginous Rameses Revenge (in Forbidden Kingdom) and the Extreme Games Zone (in Mystic East).

For something less frenetic, visit nearby **Epsom Common** (epsom-ewell.gov.uk, rail: Epsom), one of the largest stretches of rugged country within Greater London's urban limits. It's a great spot for a run-around and a wildlife watch.

Legoland

Winkfield Rd, Windsor, SL4 4AY, legoland.co.uk. Apr-Oct daily, times vary. £41.40, £31.20 child, under 3s free, online reductions. Rail: Windsor. This theme park is nominally about Lego but, although there are giant models strewn

Getting the bird at Chessington.

> **❝ ❞**
> I love Legoland because it is very fun and the rides are brilliant! I feel really excited when I go.
>
> **Talia, aged seven**

Legoland.

154

around the entire site, it's really about the 55 different rides and attractions, which range from the new undersea adventure to mini hot-air balloon rides, interactive rides (in the Traffic zone), Pirates Landing (with a swinging pirate ship) and rollercoaster rides for all ages: the Dragon's Apprentice is suitable for toddlers, while the Dragon, which swings and lurches through a castle, is restricted to children over 1.3 m. The park gets very busy in mid-summer, when queues can be painfully long and crowds oppressive.

Windsor Castle.

Thorpe Park

Staines Rd, Chertsey, KT16 8PN, T0871-663 1673, thorpepark.com. £39, £26.40 under 12s, children under 1 m free, £105.60 family (substantial reductions online). Thorpe Park's white-knuckle rides are aimed at older children. They include the Storm Surge, a 64-ft ultra-rapid, spiralling water slide, the SAW Alive horror (not for under 12s), based on the gory films of the same name, in which mutilated actors have you screaming through a labyrinth of blood-smeared rooms, the Nemesis inferno rollercoaster and the Slammer free-fall ride. There are a few concessions to smaller children: the Chief Ranger's carousel roundabout and Wet Wet Wet, a gentler water ride exclusively for families and young kids.

Whipsnade Zoo is fun and kids like me love to see animals. When I go there it makes me feel free to see nature.

Ava, aged eight

Whipsnade Zoo

Dunstable, LU6 2LF, T01582-872171, zsl.org. Daily from 1000, closing times vary, closed 25 Dec. £15.20-17.70, £12.20-13.20 child, under 3s free, 10% discount for families online. Other than Longleat, no zoo in Britain gives animals more space to roam free than Whipsnade. Here large mammals, which include all the big African species, wander around in enclosures that resemble as closely as possible their native environment. Whipsnade covers an astonishing 6000 acres, which can be explored on foot (wandering with herds of deer and bands of bouncing wallabies), by car (for an extra fee), on the zoo's narrow-gauge railway or by open-top bus. The park also has a great play area for kids and several restaurants.

Windsor Castle

Windsor, SL4 1NJ, T020-7766 7304, royalcollection.org.uk. Jan-Feb daily 0945-1500, Mar-Oct daily 0945-1600, Nov-Dec daily 0945-1500, closed 9 and 11 Apr, 14 Jun, 24-26 Dec, times vary so check website. £16.50, £9.90 child, under 5s free, £43.50 family (discounts when the state apartments are closed). Rail: Windsor Central or Windsor & Eton Riverside. Windsor is the largest and longest-occupied castle in the world. It's one of the Queen's favourite homes and she likes to spend much of her time here. The castle itself is not as swashbuckling or fairy-tale as Bodiam or Leeds (see page 167), which are both more interesting for kids. It is austere from the outside and opulent within, decorated with hundreds of priceless Gainsboroughs, Canalettos, van Dycks, Holbeins and Rembrandts from the Royal Collection, and redolent with history. Ten monarchs, including the Queen's father and mother are buried in the spectacular vaulted Gothic St George's chapel; George IV partied in the lavish semi-state rooms and sniffed flowers in the lovely rose garden. Children will be fascinated by Queen Mary's Doll's House, a perfect Palladian townhouse, which it took 1500 craftsmen – and artists, including Edwin Lutyens, three years to complete. It is accurate in every minute detail, with electric lighting, hot and cold running water and even flushing lavatories. Kids will also enjoy the great kitchens (which can only be visited on guided tours). The castle does its best to be child friendly; there are family activity trails to help kids engage with the castle's history, an interactive family audio tour and a programme of family workshops and activities during school holidays and at weekends.

The castle's massive presence hulks over the town of Windsor, looming as large as Gormenghast at every turn. The town is a rather ugly pedestrianized assemblage of shops bursting with tacky souvenirs and a few twee streets of 18th-century houses that clamber up the hill and cluster around the Thames. Also here is **Eton College** (Eton High St, SL4 6DW, T01753-671177, etoncollege.com, guided tours Wed, Fri and Sun or daily during school hols 1400 and 1515, £6.50, £5.50 child), the vast, 600-year-old public school. Visits take in the school yard (which was used as a location for Hogwarts in the Harry Potter films and for the Cambridge court race in *Chariots of Fire*), the 15th-century chapel, one of the oldest classrooms in the world and the museum of Eton life (complete with birch rods and a mock-up of a Victorian boy's room).

Woburn Safari Park

Woburn, MK17 9QN, T01525-290407, woburn.co.uk. Opening times vary, consult the website. From £12.95, from 10.95 concessions, from £8.95 child, under 3s free, family discounts available online.

Woburn, like Whipsnade, tries to emulate an African safari experience. Visitors can drive through large enclosures in their own vehicles (keep the windows wound up when there are monkeys about), take foot safaris past squirrel monkeys, meerkats and lemurs, or catch a small train, which passes through just a fraction of the park, but which is great for kids with tired legs. There is an excellent kids' play area with an animal theme and cafés.

More family favourites

Bocketts Farm Park

Young St, Fetcham, KT22 9BS, T01372-363764, bockettsfarm.co.uk. Daily 1000-1730, closed 25-26 Dec and 1 Jan. £8.25, £7.75 concessions, £6.25 2-year-olds, under 2s free. Rail: Leatherhead.

Bocketts is a working farm with animals to pet, play areas and daily events, including tractor rides, goat milking and piglet races.

Chislehurst Caves

Caveside Close, Old Hill, Chislehurst, BR7 5NL, T020-8467 3264, chislehurst-caves.co.uk. Guided tours only Wed-Sun 1000-1600, daily during school hols. £5, £3 child. Rail: Chislehurst.

The caves are a honeycomb of tunnels and caverns that were dug for chalk and brick-making in medieval times and since used as smugglers' caves, an arsenal (in the Great War) and as an air raid shelter for some 15,000 people during the Blitz. In the 1960s they were used as underground music venues for skiffle and rock 'n' roll bands. Note that toddlers might find the lamp-lit tours of the dark passageways a little too spooky.

Down House

Luxted Rd, Downe, BR6 7JT, english-heritage.org.uk. Daily 1100-1600. £9.30, £4.70 child, £23.30 family. The home of Charles Darwin has been recreated as if he were still living in it and can be combined with a visit to **Downe Bank Nature Reserve** (kentwildlifetrust.org.uk). The grassland valley is ringed with thick woods, bursting with beautiful wild flowers (including ultra-rare orchids and dropwort), buzzing with honey bees and busy with thousands of butterflies in spring and summer. It inspired the poetic last paragraph of Darwin's *The Origin of Species*, which summarized his theory of evolution by natural selection.

Drusilla's

Alfriston Rd, Alfriston, BN26 5QS, T01323-874101, drusillas.co.uk. Summer daily 1000-1800, winter daily 1000-1700. £17-29 (depending on day and month). Rail: Seaford. This delightful small theme park, set at the foot of the rolling downs 30 minutes' drive from Brighton, is like a mini-Chessington with gentler rides, soft play areas and smaller crowds. There are plenty of animals too, including Sulawesi macaques, lemurs, squirrel monkeys, caotimundis, capybaras, bear cats and the inevitable meerkats.

Hastings & Battle

www.visit1066country.com. Although it's rather frayed and run-down at the fringes, Hastings has an attractive old centre, a very good **aquarium**

Oxford & Cambridge

Wander the magnificent colleges, some dating back to the 13th century, where a string of the western world's great names have studied, including Newton, Byron, Milton, Darwin, Adam Smith and Bill Clinton, not forgetting the inventor of bossa nova, Vinicius de Moraes. Oxford is a bustling city, whereas Cambridge is a small, pretty town, dominated by the university. Its grandest college is 16th-century **Trinity College** (trin.cam.ac.uk), famous for its Great Court. The fan-vaulted chapel at **King's College** (kings.cam.ac.uk) is perhaps the most magnificent building in either Oxford or Cambridge. In Oxford, visit the **Bodleian Library** (bodleian.ox.ac.uk), the Great Hall at **Christchurch**, which features in the Harry Potter movies, and the anthropological **Pitt Rivers Museum** (prm.ox.ac.uk). And, after a look around, take the kids for a punt either along Oxford's River Cherwell, or better still down Cambridge's far prettier Cam to the lovely Grantchester Meadows. Cambridge is reached from King's Cross (60-90 mins); Oxford from Paddington (70-90 mins).

(Rock-A-Nore Rd, Sussex TN34 3DW, T01424-718776, bluereefaquarium.co.uk, daily Mar-Oct 1000-1700, Nov-Feb 1000-1600, £7.95 adult, £5.95 child, £30.75 family of 5, bluereefaquarium.co.uk), which showcases British marine wildlife, including rare sharks. The town is most famous for the battle of 1066, which wasn't fought here but rather seven

miles inland at **Battle**, which has a historic abbey and a small museum (T01424-775705, english-heritage.org.uk).

Hollycombe Steam Collection

Iron Hill, Liphook, GU30 7LP, T01428-724900, hollycombe.co.uk. Apr-Sep daily 1300-1800, but check website. £11, £9 child. Rail: Liphook. This is a magical steam-powered fairground, filled with Edwardian roundabouts, steam yachts, traction engines and dozens of locomotives of every shape and size.

Paradise Wildlife Park

White Stubbs Lane, Broxbourne, EN10 7QA, T01992-470490, pwpark.com. £12, £8 child, £38 family, extra to meet the animals.

This zoo allows children to meet many of the animals, from cuddly chinchillas to meerkats and red pandas. All sessions are supervised by keepers and the more dangerous animals like big cats are safely off limits. Parents with phobias can face them by being coaxed into handling snakes, rodents and even tarantulas.

Romney Marsh

Visitor Centre, Dymchurch Rd, New Romney, TN28 8AW, T01797-369487, kentwildlifetrust.org.uk. Apr-Sep Fri-Tue 0900-1700, Oct-Mar Sun-Mon and Fri 0900-1630.

The 27-acre marshland wildlife reserve, is home to scores of rare birds, reptiles and amphibians. There's an excellent child-friendly visitor centre (made from straw bales) and the wonderful **Romney, Hythe &**

Dymchurch Railway (rhdr.org. uk), which runs from Hythe or Dungeness to the reserve between April and September. This miniature steam railway is the world's longest 15-in gauge. Kids will love the model train sets at New Romney Station, which include one of the largest in the world.

Sheffield Park & Garden

Sheffield Park, Uckfield, TN22 3QX, T01825-790231, nationaltrust.org.uk. Jan-Feb Sat-Sun 1030-1600, Mar-Oct Tue-Sun 1030-1800, Nov-Dec Tue-Sun 1000-1600. £8.60, £4.30 child.

This gorgeous, informal 18th-century landscape garden is coloured by brilliant splashes of colour from daffodils and bluebells in spring, myriad hues of rhododendrons and azaleas in early summer and the rich reds and golden browns of hundreds of rare trees in autumn. The garden was designed by Capability Brown and adapted by Arthur G Soames in the 20th century around four centrepiece lakes and abuts a semi-wild stretch of historic parkland with stunning views.

Combine your visit with a ride on the **Bluebell Railway**

(Sheffield Park Station, TN22 3QL, T01825-720800, bluebell-railway.com, £13 return, £7 single adult, £6.50 return, £3.50 single child, £30 family), which has been running steam trains in the rolling green Wealden countryside between beautiful Sheffield Park and Kingscote for 50 years; buses continue the service through to East Grinstead or Haywards Heath.

Wakehurst Place

Ardingly, Haywards Heath, RH17 6TN, T01444-894066, nationaltrust. org.uk. Mar-Oct daily 1000-1800, Nov-Feb daily 1000-1630. £11, under 16s free.

These beautiful gardens are the National Trust's most visited property and one of the most popular with children. The gardens, which stretch around a beautiful Elizabethan mansion, are a great adventure playground for kids, who love to rush along the paths and romp in the woodland, clamber over the sandstone rocks and explore the marshy areas around the lake with their towering reeds and exotic bog plants. Wakehurst is also home to Kew's Millennium Seed Bank, which currently preserves the seeds of 10 per cent of the world's plant species for the future; it is aiming to conserve a quarter by 2020.

I think Paradise Park is fantastic! You can buy a pack of food to feed the amazing lovely animals. In the park they have some sea animals and land animals and if you don't like animals that much you can go to the shops or there is a brilliant huge park which is really special too.

Nicola, aged 11

Captivating cathedrals

Canterbury (cantweb.co.uk) is arguably Britain's most beautiful cathedral and has the country's best medieval stained glass and a magnificent spire that looks like a mandala from below. Kids will love the tomb of the Black Prince, in jet black stone, clutching a sword to his breast. Others worth visiting in the southeast include **Arundel** (arundelcathedral.org), **Chichester** (chichestercathedral.org.uk), **Ely** (elycathedral.org), **Rochester** (rochestercathedral.org) and **St Albans** (stalbanscathedral.org).

Let's go to...

Brighton

Brighton and its twin city of Hove together comprise one of Southeast England's newest and most vibrant coastal resorts. It's a popular day trip from London, especially on a sunny summer Sunday when it heaves with people. The town beach is nothing special – miles of little round pebbles washed by a cold, iron-grey sea – but there are several beachfront playgrounds and plenty of other seaside attractions for kids.

Get your bearings
Brighton railway station (Queens Rd, BN1 3XP, T0845-1272920, nationalrail.co.uk) has at least three trains an hour to London railway stations (Victoria, London Bridge and Clapham Junction) and other services to Lewes and along the coast to Southampton. The seafront and pier are 10 minutes' walk, and taxis and buses leave for destinations throughout the city from immediately outside the station. For details consult buses.co.uk or call T01273-886200. For tourist information see the Visit Brighton website (visitbrighton.com).

Town & beach
The **Palace Pier** (T01273-609361, brightonpier.co.uk, children's rides Mon-Fri 1200-1700, Sat-Sun 1100-2000) is the only surviving cast-iron Victorian pier in the city (after the West Pier burnt down mysteriously in 2003) and has a string of tacky rides, slot machines, a ghost train and a small rollercoaster. Brighton's **Sealife Aquarium** (Marine Pde, BN2 1TB, T01273-604234, visitsealife.com, daily 1000-1700, £9.50, £5.15 under 14s, £27 family) is one of the best in the country, with more than 150 species and

60 displays, including a shark and ray tank with a walk-through tunnel, piranhas, a fascinating seahorse exhibit and touch tanks. From the aquarium, you can catch the tiny **Volks Railway** (whitstablepier.com/volks, summer only Mon-Fri 1015-1700, Sat-Sun 1015-1800, every 15 mins, £1.90 single/£3 return, £1/£1.50 child) to the marina (two miles or so east of the city centre), from where it's a 20-minute walk along the cliff path to an area of plentiful **rock pools** below pretty chalk cliffs. The Volks, which rumbles along at little more than a walking pace, is the world's oldest operating electric railway; children have been riding its tiny open-sided carriages since 1883. Back in town, the seafront

is lined with rows of smart 18th-century townhouses and a splendid mock-Indian fantasy palace, the **Royal Pavilion** (Pavilion Buildings, BN1 1EE, T0300-029 0900, royalpavilion.org.uk, Oct-Mar daily 1000-1715, Apr-Sep daily 0930-1745, closed 24-26 Dec, £9.80, £7.80 concessions, £5.60 child, free under 5s), which never fails to fascinate children. It was built by John Nash (who also redesigned parts of central London, see

pages 45 and 88) for England's greatest debauchee, George IV, who was reputedly so fat that he had to have a semi-circle cut out of his dining table. The little winding **laines** (sic) and the **north lanes**, both of which run between the railway station and the sea, are great for shopping: the former for jewellery and alternative fashion and the latter for second-hand goods and music. There is a lively club scene at the weekends, when teenagers from all over Sussex flood in to the city.

Around Brighton

Families planning on spending a long weekend in Brighton will find plenty of other attractions nearby. In addition to the **South Downs** (see page 152), which begin within the city limits, there are the castle towns of **Arundel** (arundel.org.uk; see page 166) and **Lewes** (lewes.co.uk), the latter of which hosts the country's largest and most devoutly anti-Catholic bonfire night, and is home to several nature reserves. The most spectacular of these are the shingly beaches, estuarine meadows and towering white cliffs at **Cuckmere Haven** (sevensisters.org.uk, bus every 30 mins from Brighton seafront taking 40-60 mins), near the idyllic, chocolate-box village of **Alfriston** (alfriston-village.co.uk, see also Drusilla's, page 157).

Roaming for Romans

The southeast was the gateway to Roman Britain and is cluttered with Roman remains, many of which can easily be visited in a day trip from London. Highlights include the following:

Bignor Roman Villa (Bignor, near Pulborough, RH20 1PH, T01798-869259, bignorromanvilla.co.uk, Mar-Oct daily 1000-1700, Jun-Aug daily 1000-1800, £5.50, £2.50 child, £14 family) is a magnificent ruined Roman house and farm, whose cloisters preserve the longest section of Roman mosaic in the country. The museum has hundreds of Roman artefacts and the farm has animals that kids can pet, feed and ride.

Canterbury Roman Museum (Longmarket, Butchery Lane, Canterbury, CT1 2JR, T01227-785 575, canterbury.gov.uk, Mon-Sat 1000-1600, Sun 1100-1500, closed bank hols, £3.10, £2.10 child, £8 family, rail: Canterbury East) has original Roman mosaics, reconstructions of a Roman market place, complete with shops and stalls, Roman homes recreated in minute detail and a hands-on area where kids can handle real Roman objects and learn how archaeologists unearth and preserve them.

Chichester still has large sections of massively fortified third- and fourth-century Roman walls, most easily seen in the southwest corner of the city. There are also remains of a Roman mosaic in the cathedral and part of an earth amphitheatre between Eastgate and Whyke Lane. Nearby is **Fishbourne Roman Palace Museum** (Salthill Rd, Fishbourne, Chichester, PO19 3QR, T01243-785859, sussexpast.co.uk, Feb and Nov daily 1000-1600, Mar-Oct daily 1000-1700, Dec and Jan Sat-Sun 1000-1600, closed Christmas, £7.90, £4.20 child, under 5s free, rail: Fishbourne), which preserves the remains of the largest domestic Roman building so far to have been found in Britain. Kids can marvel at the spectacular mosaic floors, run around the formal garden (re-planted to its original Roman design) and see the bones of a sophisticated Roman underfloor heating system. **Lullingstone Roman Villa** (Lullingstone Lane, Eynsford, DA4 0JA, T0870-3331181, english-heritage.org.uk, daily 1000-1600, £5.90, £3 child, £14.80 family, rail: Eynsford) has superb mosaics, wall paintings and a museum filled with artefacts, including some grisly skeletal remains. The site caters well for children with plenty of hands-on stuff, including the chance to try on Roman clothes.

Richborough Fort (off Richborough Rd, Sandwich, CT13 9JW, english-heritage.org.uk, summer daily 1000-1700, £5.50, £2.30 child, rail: Sandwich) is where legions were stationed to watch over and protect the coast near Sandwich, which was frequently attacked during the Saxon invasions. The huge, crumbling stone walls surround a series of grassy ditches. Nearby **Reculver Fort** (Reculver, near Margate, CT6 6SS, english-heritage.org.uk, free, rail: Herne Bay or Birchington-on-Sea) has similarly huge walls surrounding the eerie ruins of a 12th-century church, next to a gorgeous sandy beach. The two make a great beach and history summer day out from London.

The Roman Painted House

(New St, Dover, CT17 9AJ, T01304-203279, theroman paintedhouse.co.uk, Apr-Oct usually Tue-Sat 1000-1630 but times vary, £3, £2 child, rail: Dover Priory) preserves some of the most complete remains of a Roman *mansio* guesthouse in Britain, with 400 sq ft of unique wall paintings (the most extensive so far discovered north of the Alps), the remnants of castle walls and many artefacts and remains.

Verulamium Museum

(St Michael's St, St Alban's, AL3 4SW, T01727-751810, stalbansmuseums.org.uk, Mon-Sat 1000-1730, Sun 1400-1730, £3.80, £2 child, £10.20 family, rail: St Albans) is one of the best Roman museums in Britain, with recreated rooms, a series of beautiful original paintings and mosaics and hands-on discovery and video areas aimed specifically at children. Every second week, actors dressed as Roman soldiers demonstrate the weapons, tactics and costumes of the Roman army in the museum grounds.

Let's go to...

Southend-on-Sea

Southend (visitsouth end.co.uk) is the closest seaside resort to London and, unlike Brighton, offers a series of long sandy beaches, with gentle, if cold waves.

Get your bearings
Southend Victoria railway station (Victoria Av, SS2 6AZ, T0845-6014873, nationalrail. co.uk) is 300 m from the seafront and has at least seven trains an hour to London Liverpool Street. First (firstgroup.com/ ukbus) and Arriva (arrivabus. co.uk) buses leave from outside the station for routes in and around Southend city and to nearby towns. Southend Central station (Clifftown Rd, SS1 1AB, T0845-601487, nationalrail.co.uk) is even closer to the waterfront and has at least six services an hour to London Fenchurch Street and along the Essex coast. For tourist information, see visitsouthend.co.uk.

Beaches
Despite its proximity to the capital, Southend's beaches are some of the cleanest in the southeast, with three Blue Flags and seven Quality Coast Awards. Shingly **Jubilee Beach** is the closest to the pier and is a good spot for walking dogs. **Three Shells Beach**, right on the town seafront, is great for sandcastles, with firm moist sand. There's a decent kids' play area here, climbing frames and a paddling pool. The beach gets very crowded in school holidays and at weekends, when the long, narrow sands of **Chalkwell Beach** (just south of the town centre), **Westcliff** and **Shoebury East** (which is crowned with a grassy headland) are quieter and are great spots to let kids run riot or simply wander free with a bucket and spade. Southend's pretty western suburb of **Leigh-on-Sea** (leigh-on-sea.com) has still more beaches, notably **Bell Wharf Beach**, whose calm waters make it a favourite with families.

Attractions
There's plenty more for children besides beaches. **Southend Pier** (southendpier.com) is said to be the longest pleasure pier in the world. It's little more than a jetty for much of its length: just boards and railings stretching for just over a mile to the pier head, where there's an RNLI lifeboat depot and gift shop, a small café, great views and lots of fresh sea air. A miniature electric train runs the length of the pier, taking around 10 minutes to reach the pretty glass railway station. If it rains on the esplanade, retreat to the **Sea-Life Centre** (Eastern Esplanade, SS1 2ER, T01702-442200, sealifeadventure.co.uk, opening times vary, £9, £6 under 14s, under 3s free) has some 50 tanks, including a walk-through shark tank, a deep-water display and a collection of venomous creatures. The Beach Walk exhibit showcases 120 species that can be found in the Thames Estuary; Rockpool lets kids catch crabs and touch anemones, and Sea Life Nursery is an educational conservation zone where the aquarium nurtures baby sharks and newly hatched fry. Other indoor attractions include **Kids Kingdom** (Garon Park, Eastern Av, SS2 4FA, T01702-464747, kidskingdom-southend.co.uk, under-12s only, opening times vary, £1.50-6.25 child), an enormous adventure play centre, and the **Planetarium** (Central Museum, Victoria Av, SS2 6ES, T01702-434449, southendmuseums.co.uk, Wed-Sat 1100, 1400 and 1600, £3.95, £2.95 child, £11 family) which has shows and talks aimed at children over seven. The town also has a popular theme park, **Adventure Island** (Sunken Gardens, Western Esplanade, T01702-443400, adventureisland.

co.uk). There's no entry fee, as prices are calculated on a seasonal wristband rate, so adults can come along for the day without having to pay to come along for the ride. The park is seldom crowded and, although the rollercoasters and slammers are less exhilarating than those at Thorpe Park or Chessington, most five- to 12-year-olds will find them just as fun.

Essex coast

Essex has a string of other beach towns easily reachable by rail from London. **Burnham-on-Crouch** (burnham.org.uk) is a quiet, historic village with dozens of listed buildings. It sits on the banks of a muddy estuary flanked by marshes that are visited by thousands of migrating birds in the autumn and winter. The town hosts the biggest sailing show on the east coast, starting on the August bank holiday weekend. Further north is **Clacton-on-Sea** (clacton-on-sea-essex.co.uk), a mini-Southend with long sandy beaches, a pleasure pier with rides and arcades and a fun fair. The lively Clacton carnival is held in mid-August, followed by a famous air show at the end of the month, showcasing historic British aircraft. The town's West Cliff theatre (westcliffclacton.org) is one of the few in Britain still to host an old-style family variety show every summer.

Leeds Castle.

Cool castles

The southeast has some spectacular castles, which are every bit as romantic as Windsor (see page 155) and the Tower of London (see page 80) but far less visited. Here are a pick of the best:

Arundel Castle (Arundel, BN18 9AB, arundelcastle.org, daily 1000-1700, prices vary by season, rail: Arundel) sits perched high on a hill in rolling Sussex countryside, above the impossibly pretty village-sized city of the same name. It has been a romantic retreat of the dukes of Norfolk for over 700 years and is filled with priceless antiques and works of art. Kids will be more interested in the battlements, the portcullis, moat and drawbridge. There are wonderful views from the highest walls and an activity guide for children aged five and over. The castle holds a joust and medieval week in late July.

Bodiam Castle (Bodiam, near Robertsbridge, TN32 5UA, T01580-830196, nationaltrust.org.uk, mid-Feb to Oct daily 1030-1700, Nov to mid-Dec Wed-Sun 1100-1600, early Jan-early Feb Sat-Sun 1100-1600, £6.80, £3.40 child, £18 family) is a story-book castle, with proper ramparts, round towers, tiny windows the right size for shooting arrows, a portcullis and wide moat. Inside, children can get dizzy rushing up and down spiral staircases and battlements. There are costumed historical interpreters in the courtyard daily from April to October to help contribute to the make-believe.

Colchester Castle & Museum

(Castle Park, Colchester, CO1 1YG, T01206-283931, colchestermuseums.org.uk, Mon-Sat 1000-1700, Sun 1100-1700, £6, £3.80 child, £16 family, rail: Colchester Town) is the largest Norman castle in Britain. It looks like an ungainly, lumpy church, topped with an inelegant tower and bisected by a heavy wooden walkway. But it's worth visiting for the excellent museum, which covers some 2000 years of history in the city of Colchester, including its heyday as the Roman capital of Britain, the sacking of the city by Queen Boudica, the invasion by the Normans and the siege of the castle during the Civil War.

Dover Castle

(Harold's Rd, Dover, CT16 1HU, T01304-211067, english-heritage.org.uk, Apr-Oct daily 1000-1800, Nov-Mar daily 1000-1600, £13.90-16, £7-9.60 child, £34-41.60 family, rail: Dover Priory) is every bit as magnificent and impressive as the port town is tawdry and tired. It has three rings of huge battlements, a towering, seemingly impregnable keep and superb views out across the Channel as far as France. The castle oozes history from every crenulated wall and bulwark. There are Iron Age remains, the ruins of a Pharos lighthouse built by the Romans and an Anglo-Saxon

fortress. The main castle buildings date from the 12th century, when the castle keep was the largest in Britain, grander even than the Tower of London. Beneath the castle is a vast network of tunnels, dug during the Napoleonic wars and extended in the Second World War to co-ordinate military operations like Dunkirk. Kids will enjoy the spooky tunnel tours (every 20 mins) and the calendar of activities, which include ghost tours and a medieval knight's school.

Herstmonceux Castle

(near Hailsham, BN27 1RN, T01323-834444, herstmonceux-castle. com, mid-Apr to Oct daily 1000-1800, £6, £3 child, £14 family) is a magnificent 16th-century moated castle that sits in extensive Elizabethan gardens and thick woodland. A large astronomical observatory just outside the castle grounds (the-observatory.org) makes the most of air that is some of the cleanest and least light-polluted in southeast England. The castle hosts a spectacular medieval festival (mgel.com) with jousting and battle re-enactments in late August.

Hever Castle

(Hever, near Edenbridge, TN8 7NG, T01732-865224, hevercastle.co.uk, Apr-Oct daily 1030-1700 – castle from 1200 – reduced hours in winter, £14, £12 concessions, £8 child, £36 family, rail: Edenbridge Town or Hever) is one of the country's prettiest and most romantic castles: a fortified stately home sitting in a square double moat and surrounded by lovely hedged gardens overflowing with over-the-top topiary and coloured by blooming roses and flowering shrubs. It was the childhood home of Anne Boleyn. There are numerous activities in a busy annual calendar, including jousting, May Day celebrations and family days.

Leeds Castle

(Maidstone, Kent, ME17 1PL, T01622-765400, leeds-castle.com, daily 1020-1600, £17.50, £10 child, under 4s free, rail: Bearsted) is simply one of the loveliest castles in Europe. The stately stone mansion sits within heavily fortified walls and is reflected in a lake-sized moat, surrounded by beautiful daffodil-filled gardens, dotted with huge oaks and beeches. The castle was built by the Normans and added to by many aristocrats and royals since, including Edward I and Henry VIII.

Lego parents enjoying a break.

Grown-ups' stuff London

Online resources

The city's official tourism department, **Visit London** (visitlondon.com) has an excellent website providing information on attractions and the latest round of festivals, theatre shows, performances and events.

London Families (londonfamilies.co.uk) offers ideas for family things to do in London, with a useful list of shops and a special kids' section.

Inroads

Getting there & around
London is one of the world's transport hubs, with five airports, countless railway stations serving the whole of Britain, and the UK's biggest coach station at Victoria, so arriving here from anywhere is straightforward. London's network of underground trains (subway/metro), rail, light rail, buses, river boats and trams

covers every corner of the city 24 hours a day and allows visitors to arrive at the front door of almost every attraction listed in the book. As an alternative, the London cycle hire scheme has introduced bike docking stations throughout the city (see page 172) and cycle paths within the parks are quite safe enough for kids, although extreme caution should be exercised on London's busy roads. For information on river transport, see page 22.

Transport for London (T020-7222 1234, tfl.gov.uk) has an excellent website with details of everything you could possibly want to know about the tube, overground urban rail, buses, boats, trams and cycles. The journey-planner facility allows you to work out how to get from A – be it a postcode, transport hub, attraction or important address – to B; it will even factor in walking time and plot you a

cycle route. Tourist and/or travel information booths at the major London terminus railway stations and all the Heathrow airport terminals provide pamphlets and information. Underground stations issue free tube maps and most will hand out a London transport map that also plots overground train routes.

London underground
London's underground railway has 12 colour-coded lines which extensively cover the city except for a large patch in the southeast. Routes are easy to plan using an underground station map available at all tube stations and always displayed in the stations, on the platforms and on the trains. London's transport system is grouped into nine zones. Zones 1 and 2 cover the city centre and almost all the major sights you are going to want to see. The regional sights extend to the outer zones but almost none are beyond Zone 4. A flat fee for an adult single tube journey within Zones 1 to 3 is £4, £5 for zone 6 and £7 for zone 9, so prices can mount.

Travelcards & Oyster cards
The cheapest way to negotiate London by public transport is with a Travel or Oyster card. Travelcards are combination passes that serve for the tube, bus, rail and tram. They are available for periods of one day, three days, one week, one

month and any longer period up to a year. Travelcards of varying price can be bought to cover a combination of transport zones. Prices for a Zones 1-2 card from January 2011 are as follows: one day (£8), one day off-peak – ie outside the busiest hours (£6.60), weekly (£27.60) and monthly (£106). A passport photo and ID are required to buy a weekly or monthly Travelcard. **Oyster cards** are blue plastic pre-paid smart cards. Touch them on an electronic sensor when you pass in *and out* of a tube or railway station and when you board a bus (the pad is on the driver's booth). Oysters are always cheaper than a single fare and no pricier than a one-day Travelcard. For instance, single fares within Zone 1 with an Oyster are £1.90 (as compared to £4). And, no matter how many journeys you make in any given day the fare will always be capped at the Travelcard prices. However, weekly Travelcards offer a better deal than Oyster, so use these if you intend staying in London for more than three days.

Buses & trams Although buses can be slow in heavy traffic, their network covers the entire city and travelling by bus with children is far airier and more pleasant than the tube, especially outside the city centre. Use the Transport for London website to plot a bus route for shorter journeys. Buses charge a flat single rate of £2.20 cash or £1.30 with an Oyster. There is a daily Oyster card price cap of £4. You can also buy passes which can be used exclusively on buses and trams. These offer great deals costing £17.80 for a weekly pass and £68.40 for a monthly pass. Trams operate a similar system but presently only run in the far south of the city – around Croydon, an area with few tourist attractions.

Child concessions The good news is that there are lots of concessions for kids. Most importantly, **children under 16** travel free on buses and pay half price on the tube and DLR, while **children under 11** travel free on the tube, buses, trams and DLR, when with a paying adult, and pay concessionary rates on rail and riverboats. **Young people aged 16 to 18** can obtain a Zip Oyster card which entitles them to seven-day, monthly and longer period Travelcards at child rate and half-price pay-as-you-go fares on the tube, DLR and rail. They can also get one-third off the off-peak daily price cap with a 16-25 Young Person's Railcard. Holders of Gold Card, Network Railcard, Family and Friends Railcard or an HM Forces Railcard can buy a Zones 1-9 Off-Peak Day Travelcard after 1000 for £2 and include up to four children aged up to 15.

Taxis Black cabs are the world's oldest taxi service. They are known as Hackney Carriages because they took over from the horse carriages of the same name. Black cabs are large diesel-powered cars with ample space in the back for luggage and up to four passengers. They can be hailed on the street or found at ranks outside Heathrow airport (though not Luton or Gatwick), railway stations and big hotels. An illuminated yellow 'Taxi' light on the front of the cab indicates if they are free. All fares start at £2.20 but the final fare depends on a combination of factors, including time spent in the cab, time of day and speed,

so watch that meter: prices can soar. There's a minimum airport transfer fee of £45 and a £40 fine for vomiting, which is aimed at drunks rather than babies. Cabs can be ordered over the phone or online (londonblack-cab.com) for around 10% on top of the meter fee.

Mini-cabs are far cheaper, licensed private cars which cannot be hailed; they must be pre-booked. They have broom-cupboard-sized offices all over London, especially near tube stations in outer boroughs. Quality and price varies hugely. Be sure to negotiate a price before getting into the car and exercise caution if travelling alone. Most restaurants, pubs and clubs can recommend a trustworthy local mini-cab company; a few will even ring for you. The website taxinumber. com has listings or try Addison

Lee (addisonlee.com), a large, reliable company.

Cycling Contrary to popular prejudice, London is a superb city for cycling. Hills are few and generally far between, traffic courteous by international standards and too slow to be dangerous for confident, experienced riders. Even young children can cycle safely in the city's many parks. The Mayor's **cycle hire scheme** introduced almost 6000 bikes to London in 2010 and 2011. The so-called 'Boris' bikes are kept at 'docks', most of which are near tube stations. Look for the blue-and-white circular 'cycle hire' symbols. There is a fee to take the bikes (£1 per day, £5 for 7 days) and a usage charge (30 mins free, 1 hr £1, 90 mins £4, 120 mins £6, 150 mins £6, then graded to a maximum of

£50 for 24 hrs). Users pay with a debit or credit card, receive a ticket with a unique pass code and use this to unlock the bike. When you return the bike to a dock, make sure you get a 'green light and click at the end of every trip', otherwise you will continue to be charged for your journey. There's a video showing you how the scheme works on tfl.gov.uk/BarclaysCycleHire.

Bus tours

A number of companies offer bus tours of the city. **The Original London Tour** (theoriginaltour.com, £22.50 adult, £10 child, £70 family) is one of the longest established, with the widest coverage. It is the best option for families. The company run hop-on hop-off open-top bus tours of the main sights with live commentary, running on three different routes. Between them these cover the greatest choice of sights in the city centre and include the museums as well as the big royal sights, showcase attractions and buildings of state. Tickets are cheapest when booked online and usually include a river cruise. **Big Bus Tours** (bigbustours. com, £26 adult, £10 child, £62 family) run an almost identical operation and offer tickets valid for 48 hours. **Golden Tours** (goldentours.com, prices vary according to tour) offer a big range of set tours (not hop-on

Grown-ups' stuff London

hop-off), including a 10-hour 'Total London Experience' which is an exhausting whip round Crown Jewels, Household Cavalry Museum, St Paul's, London Eye and the Changing of the Guard. Their six-hour Gems of London with the Tower of London, St Paul's and a River Cruise is less tiring for families.

Walking

London is a great city for walking – with paths along the banks of the Thames and canals and plenty of quieter streets. You can plot walking routes on Walk It (walkit.com) or using the London Geographer's A-Z map book (a-zmaps.co.uk), which lists every street and which is available online and in most newsagents.

Maps

You'll find a map of the southeast of England on page 6 and one of Central London on pages 10-11. We recommend the Geographer's A-Z map book (www.a-zmaps.co.uk), which is available both online and in a mini, pocket friendly format. This shows all of London's myriad streets. Full London Transport rail maps are available online at www.tfl.gov.uk and at railway stations.

Tots to teens

London is used to children and caters very well for them. Transport is largely free for kids, almost all attractions charge less than half-price entrance for under 18s and there are stacks of restaurants and cafés with designated kids' menus. Many of the big tourist sights, like the London Dungeon, London Eye and Natural History Museum, are designed specifically for children, and those that aren't, almost invariably bear kids in mind. You can take it for granted that even the frowstiest and most highbrow of museums and galleries will have activity trails for any children old enough to read. Many, including such illustrious establishments as the Victoria and Albert and British museums, have activity backpacks stuffed with goodies guaranteed to bring the museum to life, and a good percentage have soft play areas for tots. Check the attraction's website before you reach the capital: most have designated kids' or family pages, and many offer discounts and queue-jump tickets for booking online.

Many families visiting the capital spend their time frenetically rushing from one big attraction to another: a morning cramming in the South Bank, followed by an afternoon at the Natural History Museum. They return home or to their

hotel rooms exhausted and irritable, clutching a packet of headache pills and cursing London. It's easy to avoid such affliction, first by choosing to visit only specific exhibits or galleries in the largest museums (the museum websites are invaluable for planning). Or, perhaps, by visiting a couple of smaller establishments that offer a bite-sized, easily digestible chunk of culture for kids, like the Horniman or the Sir John Soane. Secondly, remember that London has far more wide open, crowd-free spaces than it does stuffy, crammed interiors. Explore them, rest in them, allow kids to romp and roam around them and you will return from London refreshed. According to Natural England, green space makes up 60% of the London region, one of the highest percentages for any world capital. A park is never far away in London, and some have superb playgrounds. And there are waterways too: London has the Thames, the Lee, the babbling brooks of Hampstead Heath, Bushy Park and Richmond Common, glorious canals and the largest urban wetland centre in any European capital.

Babies

Most attractions in London (like the Science and Natural History museums and the London Eye) are pushchair accessible.

Those that aren't (like the Tower of London or the Horniman) usually have a 'buggy park', where pushchairs can safely be stored. Lavatories in the larger museums and attractions almost all have nappy-changing facilities, and cafés and restaurants often have high chairs. Older babies will love the zoos and aquaria. A number of cinemas have baby and family screenings. They include all the following: Picturehouse cinemas in Clapham, Notting Hill Gate, Greenwich and Brixton, all the Odeon group (through their newbie sessions), the Everyman Cinema in Hampstead, the Electric Cinema on Portobello Road and the Rio Cinema in Dalston.

Toddlers

Toddlers will enjoy London's parks, green spaces, playgrounds and city farms. Be sure to visit the London Wetland Centre, one of the excellent playgrounds and one of the smaller zoos – either Battersea Park Children's Zoo or the tiny zoo in Golders Hill Park. They will also love the active play area in the Science Museum basement, which has lots of blocks and electronic drawing games. London Toddler (londontoddler.com) is a useful internet resource.

School age

London offers so much for children aged between four

If all else fails…

Indoor adventure play areas allow kids to crawl through tubes, climb up towers, wade in vast bins filled with coloured balls and generally run amok in complete safety. **Kidspace** (kidspaceadventures.com, rail: Waddon or East Croydon) is the largest in London with the standard soft play set-up as well as a mini go-kart track, a giant climbing frame and a host of organized activities. Also try **Topsy Turvy World** (topsyturvyworld. com, tube: Brent Cross), **Play Away** (playawaylondon.co.uk, tube: Highgate or Crouch Hill), **Clown Town** (clowntown.co.uk, tube: East Finchley), **Discovery Planet** (surreyquaysshoppingcentre.co.uk, tube: Canada Water), **Eddie Katz** (eddiecatz.com, tube: Putney) or **It's a Kid's Thing** (itsakidsthing.co.uk, rail: Earlsfield).

In addition to the **BFI IMAX** (see page 32), there are **IMAX** screens (imax.com) at the **London Science Museum** (T0870-870 4868, see page 61) and at the following cinemas in the **Odeon** group (T0871-224 4007): Greenwich, Kingston, Uxbridge and Wimbledon.

Go-karting is an exciting option for older children who need to let off steam and many tracks have family times, when parents can have a spin around too. Note that tracks have an age restriction (usually between six and eight years old) and a minimum inside leg length of 25 inches; check on the websites for full details. **Go-karting London** (T08444-109109, team-sport.co.uk, £29.95, £24.95 child) has tracks in various parts of London, including Tower Bridge and Edmonton.

Toy shops

Museum shops The British Museum (see page 74), Natural History Museum (see page 62), Museum of London (see page 78), Cartoon Museum (see page 70), Design Museum (see page 39), Geffrye Museum (see page 143), V&A (see page 65), Horniman (see page 112) and Fan Museum (see page 145) all have great gift shops packed with an ever-changing selection of stuff for kids. Best of all is the **Science Museum** (see page 61), whose shop stocks an imaginative choice of books, games and creative toys, which include build-your-own robot kits, hydrophobic sand and rockets.

Benjamin Pollock's Toyshop (1st floor, Central Av, Covent Garden Piazza, WC2E 8RF, T020-7379 7866, pollocks-coventgarden.co.uk, tube: Covent Garden) is the retail outpost of Pollock's Toy Museum (see page 72). It is great for arty

kids, with a range of carefully crafted traditional toys including gorgeous model theatres (which come complete with plays), soft toys (including lovely teddy bears), dolls' houses, wooden models, books and games. Almost nothing is plastic or requires huge numbers of batteries.

Forbidden Planet (179 Shaftesbury Av, WC2H 8JR, T020-7420 3666, forbiddenplanet.com, tube: Piccadilly Circus) is one of the largest and best shopping outlets for fans of science fiction, fantasy and cult entertainment. There is simply nowhere better in Europe to buy comics and graphic novels, action figures, games, science fiction DVDs and cult collectibles. If your kids are into this kind of thing, allow hours.

Hamleys (188-196 Regent St, W1B 5BT, T0870-333 2450, hamleys. com, tube: Oxford Circus) is the

self-proclaimed greatest toy shop in the world but it offers little that is unique and much that is overpriced. It's most useful as a one-stop toyshop in a hurry, where you can pick up the latest Bionicle, Sylvanian Families set or games console, as well as old faithfuls like Rubik's cubes, Monopoly boards and radio-controlled cars. Kids love seeing the toys being demonstrated by the cool young staff but they'll hate the crowds, which get almost unbearable close to Christmas.

Honeyjam (267 Portobello Rd, W11 1LR, T020-7243 0449, honeyjam. co.uk, tube: Ladbroke Grove or Westbourne Park) is owned by booze heiress and model Jasmine Guinness. It is an earnest attempt to create a high-quality fairy-tale toyshop, crammed with desirable goodies. Toys include a lovely pirate ship and big dolls' houses, horrible

gooey dough, cupcake soaps, and soft furry rabbits, geese and bears for younger children.

International Magic (89 Clerkenweel Rd, EC1R 5BX, T020-7405 7324, internationalmagic.com, tube: Chancery Lane or Farringdon) is London's only magic shop and has been selling magic tricks, books and accessories to young magicians of all levels for more than 50 years. It also stocks tutorial DVDs and runs beginners' magic courses.

ModelZone (202 High Holborn, WC1V 7BD, T020-7405 6285, modelzone.co.uk, tube: Holborn) stocks Revell, Airfix model kits, model cars, tanks, cranes, diggers and the like, train sets, Scalextric, action figures and radio-controlled cars, planes and helicopters. The shop is usually as crammed with grown-up collectors as with kids.

It has one of the widest ranges in the country and a comprehensive online shop.

Petit Chou (15 St Christopher's Pl, W1U 1NR, T020-7486 3637, petitchou.co.uk, tube: Bond Street) is a charming, bright little shop that stocks a huge range of very well made but pricey wooden toys from all over the world, including delightful chunky London buses and black cabs, alphabet games, building blocks, music boxes and vintage pedal cars. There's a small selection of French designer clothes for kids, too, as well as soft toys and wall hangings.

Playlounge (19 Beak St, Soho, W1F 9RP, T020-7287 7073, playlounge. co.uk, tube: Oxford Circus) is a thoughtful little shop that sells a very personal collection of beautifully designed toys, books

and games. The owner, Aidan Onn, combs the world's toy fairs for quirky, odd and cute items that will be as tempting to adults as they are to kids. We love the Cubees – Japanese farm animals that stack on top of each other and spontaneously burst into cutesy singing and flapping in time to the music.

Pandemonium (125 Sheen Lane, SW14 8AE, T020-8878 0866, pandemoniumlondon.com, rail: Mortlake) is an award-winning, colourful little shop that stocks a huge range of traditional and modern toys, from scooters, wooden blocks, Airfix models and Meccano to Dr Who models and memorabilia, party games and education and science toys. The shop is great for a browse and the excellent website allows for online shopping.

and 12 that it is impossible to recommend one attraction over another. The best tactic is to base a visit on your child's key interests. London will have something which fits the bill, whether they love fans (Fan Museum) and dolls' houses (Windsor Castle), guns and planes (the army museums), dressing-up (Hampton Court, the V&A, Greenwich Discovery Centre), animals (London Zoo, Battersea Park Zoo), wildlife (the Wetland Centre, any of the larger parks), castles (the Tower of London, Windsor) or pretty much anything else. Kids who love to do nothing can lounge in a park, slob out at the cinema or snooze on a Thames cruise.

Teenagers

The world is a teenager's Oyster card in London, which will enable them to travel independent of Mum and Dad to all corners

of the city for a cut price. They will invariably find what they are looking for, be it world-class theatre and world-class shopping in the West End, music in one of a plethora of clubs or at the British Music Experience, or a hair-raising time at Chessington and the London Dungeon. Some will enjoy posing with the celebrities in wax at Madame Tussaud's or staring at the big screen in the BFI IMAX. Teenagers will also love London's museums and galleries, where it is a good idea to let them wander at whim, especially on a quieter day. The city's galleries and museums offer stacks of free or modestly priced workshops and courses aimed specifically at teenagers. They can draw or paint at the Saatchi, National or Tate galleries, play music at the Barbican and join an acting workshop at the Old Vic (oldvictheatre.com) and other theatres (see page 21). Teenagers

can also explore the city by bike or foot, walking or cycling along the Regent's and Grand Union canals or Thames Path to Windsor and seeing London shift slowly from urban to rural, mountain biking or day hiking in Epping Forest. Or they can fly kites in Alexandra Park or on Primrose Hill, go go-karting, horse riding, or jet boating on the Thames, watch a gig at one of the hundreds of live music venues or attend a summer festival… In fact, if they get tired of London, it can only be, as Dr Johnson so accurately observed, that they are tired of life.

Single parents

Single parents travelling alone won't be able to take advantage of the family ticket offers at the more expensive attractions. However, many of the city's great attractions are free, and there are so many online discounts available that single parents should be able to make savings too.

Parents of children with special needs

Transport is the single greatest difficulty in London for those with special needs, especially mobility needs. Access to tube platforms is usually by escalator (although a few stations have lifts) and most tube trains and buses are not wheelchair accessible; the newest stations and the trains on the Jubilee line between Westminster and Stratford are the exceptions. Black cabs all have wheelchair access, however. Further information can be found on the Transport for London website. Many but by no means all of the city's museums and attractions are wheelchair accessible. Big attractions which are not include the Tower of London, Kensington Palace, three of the four entrances to the Tate Britain (wheelchair access via the Atterbury St entrance) and Westminster Abbey. *Access in London: A Guide for People Who Have Difficulty Getting Around*, by Gordon Couch (Access Project), is an invaluable guide. Artsline (artsline.org.uk) is the UK's leading disability access website, providing searchable information on over 1000 arts venues across London. Disability Now (disabilitynow.org.uk) is a more general website but with many articles and links related to London.

Eating

We have the space here only to scratch the surface of the vast London restaurant scene, so for more information consult some of the excellent books and online guides to eating out in London. We like london-eating.co.uk and squaremeal.co.uk. Here we offer general advice and a broad brushstroke of restaurant areas and styles.

Chains

International fast-food chains are legion in London so you'll never be far from a fat-filled burger or doughy pizza. But they sit alongside more interesting local alternatives. In London it's a cinch to find a sumptuous salad, a piquant pepperoni-covered pizza, a wholegrain sandwich packed with organic veggies, or a brie-and-bacon-stuffed croissant that costs little

more than a fast-food burger meal. Here are some kid-friendly chains with branches throughout London:

Gallic goodies at Café Rouge (caferouge.co.uk) Café Rouge serves up French-style snacks for families, alongside staples with a Gallic veneer like minute steak with French fries and beurre fondu. Little ones get an Enfants' Menu (sic) with a safe choice of omelette, sausages, baguettes, fishcakes or pasta, and place mats to colour in. All is served in warmly lit, faux brasserie surroundings. Average price for a main £7.95; set meals for kids £5.75.

A bed for the night

London has more hotel beds than any other city in Europe and finding accommodation is rarely a problem. The best resources are online travel agents, which are far more comprehensive in their coverage than any generalist guidebook. Trip Advisor (tripadvisor.co.uk) offer full reviews of hotels of all level by people who have stayed there, a map facility showing precisely where the hotel is situated and icons showing the hotel's specialities. A button allows users to click through to a host of online booking services which offer great discounts from the rack rate. These include Expedia (expedia.co.uk), Booking.com, Ebookers (www.ebookers.com), and Hotels.com and LateRooms (laterooms.com), both of which have search filters which allow users to search for family-friendly hotels. The best plan is to choose an area you'd like to stay and a desired price bracket and then search. Be sure to select a hotel close to an underground station.

Grown-ups' stuff London

Burgers and chunky chips at Giraffe (giraffe.net) Giraffe offers comfort food in comfortable surroundings, with a menu carefully crafted for kids. There are crayons and paper to doodle on while you wait and a free plastic giraffe (which children love) with every meal. The kids' breakfast, brunch, lunch and dinner menus include fairly healthy burgers with chunky chips, pasta, ice creams and sorbets. Mains cost around £4 for kids and £10 for adults.

Gourmet Burger Kitchen (gbk. co.uk) The Gourmet Burger kitchen does what it says on the sign. Here burgers are noble not nasty, made with Aberdeen Angus beef, served in crisp, fresh buns and accompanied with slices of buffalo mozzarella, pesto and salad or sour cream, avocado and spicy kidney beans. The small fry get a special set menu with a choice of Cajun chicken pieces, puy lentils and various mini burgers accompanied by juices or milk shakes. There are more than 20 Gourmet Burger restaurants in London. Average price for a main £8.20; set meals for kids £6.25.

Turkish and Middle Eastern delights at Hummus Brothers (hbros.co.uk) This London chain is great for kids whose tastes have progressed beyond standard fare. They serve generous portions of healthy meals including hummus, falafel, guacamole, tabouleh, sautéed chicken and similar with warm pitta bread, and a range of salads and desserts. They have three branches in central London and deliver. Mains from £4.

Mild spice in the Masala Zone (masalazone.com) This small London chain takes our new national dish beyond frayed velvet, cheesy Indian scenery and piped sitar music into young, modish surrounds with retro-chic 1930s posters, soft lighting and funky furniture. Spice-shy kids should opt for a mild chicken korma, cooked in butter and coconut. There are Masala Zones in Covent Garden, Soho, Earl's Court, Islington, Fulham and Camden, and, by the time you read this, there will be half a dozen more. Average price for a main £10.

Portuguese fried chicken at Nando's (nandos.co.uk) Nando's offer snack-style chicken in sit-down restaurants decorated with splashes of Mediterranean colour and with real crockery and metal cutlery on the tables. Spiciness comes in grades: lemon and herb or Nando's Nandinos are best for kids, then there's medium, hot and extra hot for grown-ups. Drinks are bottomless, there are veggie options and service is quick and no-nonsense: just the ticket if you have hungry kids. Average price for a main £8-10.

Posh pizza at a bargain price at Pizza Express (pizzaexpress. com) Pizza Express is an absolute kids' favourite and with a branch on almost every other street, it's never hard to find. Their recipe for success is long tried and tested: Italian-style, thin-crust pizzas are prepared in an open-plan kitchen, fired in super-hot gas ovens and whisked to marble tables in a matter of minutes by courteous young staff. There's a great-value three-course Piccolo menu for kids, with thoughtful additions which make them feel like grown-up gourmets: a starter of doughballs and salad, a pizza or pasta for main, a choice of dessert and a *Bambinoccino* (made from frothy milk topped with powdered chocolate) to finish. Activity sheets and crayons are also provided. Average price for a pizza is £7; Piccolo menu £6.25. **Zizzi** (zizzi.co.uk) offer similar with more pasta options.

Waffles, crêpes and pancakes at My Old Dutch (myolddutch. com) This small chain of restaurants has been serving a broad range of sweet and savoury pancakes, waffles and Dutch poffertjes (light, fluffy baby pancakes, traditionally served with sugar and butter) for 50 years. The recipes have changed little, the restaurants are warm, bright and friendly and very popular with children. Pancakes from £7.95, poffertjes from £4.95.

Great-value Italian at Carluccio's (carluccios.com). Antonio Carluccio's restaurants offer Italian staples in homely surrounds, with a wealth of hand-made pasta and grills, a kids' three-course menu finishing with ice cream and Italian coffee and cakes. They have more than 20 restaurants in London. Average price for a main is £7, kids' menu from £6.25. **Bella Italia** (bellaitalia. co.uk) offers similar at slightly lower quality.

Sandwiches on the go at Pret a Manger (pret.com) Pret began in London and has proliferated like Starbucks. Its slick brushed-steel and chrome food bars are great for a quick bite, with a wide choice of ultra-fresh sandwiches, salads and lunchtime snacks available throughout London. Average price for a sandwich £3.50. Other sandwich shops include **Eat** (eat.co.uk).

Regional food

London is the best place in Britain for kids to try something new and sample food from all over the world. **Chinatown** (chinatownlondon.org) is based in the streets immediately north of Leicester Square, where restaurants have been serving crispy fried duck, chop suey and chow mein since the sixties; they remain as popular as ever. Most are spread along Gerrard Street and adjacent Wardour Street. Old favourites like the **Jade Garden** (15 Wardour St, W1D 3HD, T020-7437 5065) serve decent dim sum (not the frozen stuff so common in Soho) and reliable Chinese standards. Fresher, younger and more authentically Chinese newcomers like **Baozi Inn** (25 Newport Court, WC2H 7JS, T020-7287 6877) whip out Chengdu noodles in what seems like a few minutes, as well as very spicy Sichuanese dishes. Ask for guidance for kids. **Brick Lane** (visitbricklane. org) is London's curry central. The whole street is lined with Bangladeshi restaurants offering great-value, traditional British

curry fare and each fronted by a tout brandishing a menu. We like the **Bengal Village** (75 Brick Lane, E1 6QL, T020-7366 4868, bengalvillage.com), which has plenty of mild options for kids and delicious sweet lassi. Streets on and around **Hoxton Square**, 500 m further north, bristle with restaurants, including some great Vietnamese cheapies (around the Geffrye Museum), including the ever-popular **Cay Tre Vietnamese Kitchen** (301 Old St, EC1V 9LA, T020-7729 8662, vietnamesekitchen. co.uk.). There are also some great-value Japanese restaurants in London with kid-friendly menus that offer steaming udon noodles, delicious soups and sushi. **Yo Sushi** (yosushi. com), which has more than 25 restaurants in the capital, is a perennial kids' favourite, with mini dishes (colour-coded for price) spinning round the restaurant on a long conveyor belt. The much-loved noodle chain, **Wagamama** (wagamama. com) has a special kids' menu with grilled chicken or grilled fish noodles, stir fries and fruit lollies for dessert, plus a huge menu for adults. There are more than 20 branches in Central London. **Benihana** (benihana. co.uk) which has restaurants in Piccadilly and Chelsea is a US take on a traditional Japanese grill where meat and fish is cooked in front of customers on a large metal hot plate. For more authentically Japanese fare head for **Golders Green** where you will find restaurants like **Café Japan** (626 Finchley Rd, NW11 7RR, cafejapan.co.uk) and **Atari Ya** (16 Monkville Parade, Finchley Rd, NW11 0AL, atariya.co.uk), a cheap-as-chips sushi bar selling some of the freshest, finest sashimi in London. Golders Green and nearby **Hendon** are also the place for the best kosher food in the capital. The **White House** (whitehouserestaurant.co.uk) has a huge menu of steaks, Asian dishes, burgers and snacks, as well as kosher ice cream for pudding. The *London Kosher Guide* (londonkosherguide.com) offers a list of kosher restaurants all over the capital. The **Tas** chain (tasrestaurant.com), with restaurants all over London, serve good-value, well prepared halal food from a menu dominated by Turkish dishes.

Cafés, diners & fish 'n' chips

Kids seldom turn up their nose at an all-day breakfast, burgers and hot dogs or fish 'n' chips. London offers all by the plate load. Most are dreadful. Here are a few which are better and a few more which serve sophisticated modern fare for grown-ups, besides.

All Star Lanes (95 Brick Lane, E1 6QL, T020-7426 9200, allstarlanes.co.uk, with other branches in Holborn and Bayswater) is an East End take on a Mid-West American diner, serving great burgers, juices for kids, sizzling hot chilli con carne, steaks and American beer for grown-ups; there are bowling alleys for a pre- or post-meal game. Mains from £10.95, kids menus from £8.45.

Blandford's (65 Chiltern St, Marylebone, W1U 5AF, T020-7486 4117) Breakfasts don't get much better or bigger than those served at Blandford's, with Beano comic portions of eggs, bacon, beans, mushrooms, tomatoes, sausage and toast served with a steaming hot mug of tea. Perfect for kids of all ages.

The Breakfast Club (branches in Islington, Soho, Spitalfields and Hoxton, thebreakfastclub cafes.com). This café is a child's delight, with a menu stuffed with pancakes, burgers, burritos, buffalo wings, nachos, hot sandwiches, baked potatoes and breakfast until 1700. Oh, and there's sticky toffee pudding, banoffee pie, apple crumble and ice cream for afters.

Café Crescent (40 Camden High St, NW1 0JH) serves chips as thick as your wrist, baked beans by the puddle-load, perfectly cooked bacon, crisp at the edges and soft in the centre, and gooey eggs. All of which make this classic working man's café, with its plastic tablecloths and fading film posters, a London treasure that kids will adore almost as much as the cabbies who use it.

Ed's Easy Diner (edseasydiner. com) has been serving great burgers and shakes in delightful faux retro US 1950s diners for over a decade. There's a huge breakfast menu, vast sandwiches (including a great BLT), hot dogs, chicken and an excellent value kids' menu. The chain has four branches in central London. Burgers from £6.55, kids' menu from £6.30.

The Diner (with branches in Soho, Camden, Hoxton, Islington and Kensal Rise, goodlifediner. com) brings the New York diner to London. Sort of. There are plenty of very English options on the kids' menu, like sausage and mash, fish fingers, and ham and cheese omelet. There's banana split or chocolate fudge cake for afters.

Fishbone (82 Cleveland St, W1T 6NF, T020-7580 2772) serves great fish 'n' chips in a great location – close to Regent's Park. Eat in or grab a bag and head for the park but be prepared for a 10-minute wait – the cook here batters and fries each fish rather than leaving it sitting pre-fried under heatlamps.

Squat & Gobble (69 Charlotte St, W1T 4RW, T020-580 5338, squatandgobble.co.uk). This deli-cum-café produces a generous full-English brekkie until midday and all day Saturday, almost instantaneously, as well as porridge, a healthy breakfast of fruit salad with yoghurt and muesli, and good lunchtime kid-friendly staples like rib-eye steak, baked potatoes with tuna and mayo and bangers and mash.

Regency Café (17-19 Regency St, Westminster, SW1P 4BY, T020 7821 6596). This is a proper London caff, with a huge menu of essentially the same dishes, all of them somehow involving bacon, tea strong enough to revive the dying, formica tables and an atmosphere like a classic episode of Minder.

Rock & Soul Plaice (47 Endell St, WC2H 9AJ, T020-7836 3785). This shop has been serving fish 'n' chips since 1871, 1874 or World War II depending on who you ask, and is therefore either London's oldest chippy or one of them. Food is traditional fare with kids' portions available. Come in the evenings, when it's busy, for the freshest food.

Sacred (branches in Soho, Covent Garden, off Tottenham Court Rd and in the Westfield Shopping Centre, sacredcafe. co.uk). This small but growing chain brings New Zealand new cooking to the British all-day breakfast, with dishes like toasted bagels served with organic scrambled egg, spring onion and feta cheese, and organic chocolate cake served with fresh cream or unsweetened yoghurt.

Restaurants for a special occasion

Unfortunately most of London's gourmet restaurants turn up their noses at children, preferring them not to be seen, let alone heard, and it can be hard to find a place for a special treat. It's a long way from gourmet, but kids love the Rainforest Café (20-24 Shaftesbury Av, W1D 7EU, T020-

7434 3111, therainforestcafe. co.uk; book a table on bank holidays). The café is in reality the city's largest family restaurant and offers a huge menu of international dishes, including a Middle Eastern mezze, chicken satay and enchiladas served US style – with lashings of condiments and in portions the size of Texas. Kids love the restaurant for the wet and wild decor. The dining room is dominated by a huge aquarium, fake vines and bromeliads cover the walls and there is a constant wildlife soundtrack. Mains from £15.

Le Cercle (1 Wilbraham Place, Chelsea, SW1X 9AE, T020-7901 9999, www.lecercle.co.uk), is an award-winning, French, fine-dining restaurant which welcomes children and which has a menu of amuses bouches which is perfect for kids. Be sure to sample the glorious puddings. Average price for a main £30. **The Blue Elephant** (3-6 Fulham Broadway, SW6 1AA, T020-7385 6595, blueelephant. com) serves delicious Royal Thai cuisine (highlights include the aromatic salad of crispy banana flowers and prawns) in fabulous surroundings which children will love. Tinkling artificial streams are filled with koi carp, and the charming, Thai staff dressed in brilliantly coloured silks both welcome and fascinate kids. Average price for a main £20.

Picnic in the park

In sunny weather, a picnic in a London park is a real treat. Supermarkets for essential supplies are never more than a few hundred metres from a tube station (you can find a comprehensive listing through supermarket websites or sites like londononline.co.uk) but it's also worth seeking out one of London's delis for something a bit more special.

Green Park Delis and restaurants around Green Park tend to be expensive, although **Fortnum & Mason's** food hall on Piccadilly is definitely worth an ogle even if you don't plan on buying anything. A cheap and cheerful alternative is Gaby's Deli (30 Charing Cross Rd, WC2H 0DE, T020-7836 4233), a modest shop conveniently located right near Leicester Square. It offers decent snacks, sandwiches, falafels, salads, pittas stuffed with hummus and similar. Another central option is **Lina Stores** (18 Brewer St, Soho, W1F 0SH, T020-7437 6482). It's a tube ride from Green Park (via Leicester Square or Piccadilly), but it is quite simply the best Italian deli in central London with exquisite antipasti: try the sun-dried tomatoes and juicy olives, cheeses, Italian breads, salamis and cheeses (including wonderful gorgonzola).

Greenwich Park Buenos Aires Café and Delicatessen (86 Royal Hill, Greenwich, SE10 8RT, buenosairesltd.com) is a classy deli that sells great breads, meats, cheeses and cakes and doubles up as a smart café-restaurant where kids can tuck into a hearty tea or even a huge slab of steak with chips.

Hampstead Heath Rosslyn Deli (56 Rosslyn Hill, NW3 1ND, T020-7794 9210) is a multi-award winning deli 100 m south of Hampstead tube. It's a real gem, serving fine pastries, French breads, olives, one of the best selections of cheeses and cold meats in the capital as well as delicious biscuits and chocolates.

Hyde Park/Kensington Gardens The Bathurst Deli (3 Bathurst St, W2 2SD, T020-7262 1888) is less than five minutes' walk from Hyde Park and is even closer to Lancaster Gate tube station. It's a French-run deli that sells choice cheeses, crispy bread, olives, wine, juices and a range of lunches and snacks, including *empanadas*, classy pizzas and lasagne. Another good choice is **Paul** (41 Thurloe St, South Kensington, SW7 2LQ, T020-7581 6034, www.paul.fr/uk), one of a chain of upmarket French deli-bakeries and sandwich shops that is becoming increasingly popular in London. Come here to buy French apple tarts, cakes, crunchy baguettes and delicious pastries, either to take away to Hyde Park or Kensington Gardens or to eat in after a busy morning at the museums on nearby Exhibition Road.

Regent's Park Ferreira Delicatessen (40 Delancey St at Albert St, Camden Town, NW1 7RY, T020-7748 52351) is 100 m from the park and sells freshly made sandwiches, cheeses, salads, fruit, figs and freshly baked bread as well as delicious Portuguese *pastel de nata* custard tarts.

Index

Image credits

credits

Footprint credits

Project editor: Felicity Laughton
Text editor: Sophie Jones
Proofreader: Sarah Thorowgood
Layout & production: Angus Dawson, Emma Bryers
Maps: Gail Townsley

Managing Director: Andy Riddle
Commercial Director: Patrick Dawson
Publisher: Alan Murphy
Publishing Managers: Felicity Laughton, Nicola Gibbs
Digital Editor: Jo Williams, Jen Haddington
Marketing & PR: Liz Harper
Advertising: Renu Sibal, Elizabeth Taylor
Finance & administration: Elizabeth Taylor

Print

Printed in India by Replika Press Pvt Ltd

Every effort has been made to ensure that the facts in this guidebook are accurate. However, travellers should still obtain advice from consulates, airlines, etc about travel and visa requirements before travelling. The authors and publishers cannot accept responsibility for any loss, injury or inconvenience however caused.

Footprint Feedback

We try as hard as we can to make each Footprint guide as up to date as possible but, of course, things always change. If you want to let us know about your experiences – good, bad or ugly – then don't delay, go to www.footprintbooks.com and send in your comments.

Publishing information

Footprint London with Kids, 1st edition
© Footprint Handbooks Ltd, April 2011

ISBN 978-1-907263-33-0
CIP DATA: A catalogue record for this book is available from the British Library

® Footprint Handbooks and the Footprint mark are a registered trademark of Footprint Handbooks Ltd

Published by Footprint

6 Riverside Court
Lower Bristol Road
Bath BA2 3DZ, UK
T +44 (0)1225 469141
F +44 (0)1225 469461
discover@footprinttravelguides.com
footprinttravelguides.com

Distributed in North America by

Globe Pequot Press, Guilford, Connecticut

 This product includes mapping data licensed from Ordnance Survey® with the permission of the Controller of Her Majesty's Stationery Office. © Crown Copyright. All rights reserved. Licence No. 100027877.

Acknowledgements

Many thanks to Felicity, Sophie, Angus, Emma and Alan at Footprint for such grace, patience and professionalism under pressure. Great thanks also are owed to Raphael Robinson, Elizabeth Robinson (for helping so much as ever), Farhoud 'Frank by name' Farhoumand, Pete, Liz, Kiera, Saoirse and Dominic, Rob, Ana Paula, Harry and Giovanna, Damian, Leia and Oscar, Paul 'Larry London' Turner, Marcela, Gabriel, Eugenio and Ale, Behrooz, Roya, Ali and Rayan, Miguel, Carla, Rute, Ines and Hayley, Simon, Caroline and Aaron, Matt, Theo and Olivia. And last but very far from least all the staff, children and parents of Brooklands School in Hampstead Garden Suburb who contributed so much to the kids' comments.